CW00487280

THE

Christian's Secret

OF

A Happy Life

(REVISED AND ENLARGED EDITION)

Hannah Whitall Smith

Bibliographic Information

Born to a prominent Quaker family in Philadelphia, Pennsylvania in 1832, Hannah Whithall Smith was a lay speaker and author in the Holiness Movement. She married Robert Piersall Smith in 1851 and together they embarked on a speaking tour throughout the United States and in England where they experienced great success.

In 1875, she published the spiritual classic, *The Christian's Secret of A Happy Life*. The revised and enlarged edition was previously published by F. E. LONGLEY, at his depot for the English and American literature of scriptural holiness, 39, Warwick Lane, London, 1876.

Toward the end of her life, she dedicated her time to social causes and was a leader in the Women's suffrage movement. Though confined to a wheelchair, and suffering from arthritis, Hannah remained spiritually happy until her death in 1911.

an Ichthus Publications edition

Copyright © 2014 Ichthus Publications
ISBN 10: 1502363267
ISBN 13: 978-1502363268

www.ichthuspublications.com

CONTENTS

PREFACE

THIS IS NOT A THEOLOGICAL BOOK. I frankly confess I have never studied Theology, and do not understand its methods nor its terms. But the Lord has taught me experimentally and practically certain lessons out of His Word, which have greatly helped me in my Christian life, and have made it a very happy one. And I want to tell these lessons, in the best way I can, in order that some others may be helped into a happy life also. I cannot bear to keep the secret to myself.

I do not want to change the theological views of a single individual. I dare say most of my readers know far more about Theology than I do myself, and perhaps you may discover abundance of what will seem to you to be theological mistakes. But let me beg of you not to mind these. Try, instead, to get at the experimental point of that which I have tried to say, and if that is practical and helpful, forgive the blundering way in which it is expressed. Throw over it all the mantle of Christian love. Say, if you choose, "Well, she is only a woman, and cannot be expected, therefore, to understand Theology;"—but remember that God sometimes reveals, even to babes, secrets that He has hidden from the wise and prudent.

I have committed my book to the Lord, and have asked Him to counteract all in it that is wrong, and to let only that which is true find entrance into any heart. It is sent out in tender sympathy and yearning love for all the struggling weary ones in the Church of Christ, and its message goes right from my heart to theirs. I have given the best I have, and could do no more. May the blessed Holy Spirit use it to teach some of my readers the true secret of a happy life!

H. W. S.

1

INTRODUCTORY

GOD'S SIDE AND MAN'S SIDE

IN INTRODUCING THIS subject of the life and walk of faith, I
desire, at the very outset, to clear away one misunderstanding
which very commonly arises in reference to the teaching of it, and
which effectually hinders a clear apprehension of such teaching. This
misunderstanding comes from the fact that the *two* sides of the subject
are rarely kept in view at the same time. People see distinctly the way in
which one side is presented, and, dwelling exclusively upon this, without
even a thought of any other, it is no wonder that distorted views of the
whole matter are the legitimate consequence.

Now there are two very decided and distinct sides to this subject,
and, like all other subjects, it cannot be fully understood unless both of
these sides are kept constantly in view. I refer, of course, to God's side
and man's side; or, in other words, to God's part in the work of
sanctification, and man's part. These are very distinct and even
contrastive, but are not contradictory; though, to a cursory observer,
they sometimes look so.

This was very strikingly illustrated to me not long ago. There were
two teachers of this higher Christian life holding meetings in this same
place, at alternate hours. One spoke only of God's part in the work, and
the other dwelt exclusively upon man's part. They were both in perfect
sympathy with one another, and realised fully that they were each
teaching different sides of the same great truth; and this also was

understood by a large proportion of their .hearers. But with some of the hearers it was different, and one lady said to me, in the greatest perplexity, "I cannot understand it at all. Here are two preachers undertaking to teach just the same truth, and yet to me they seem flatly to contradict one another." And I felt at the time that she expressed a puzzle which really causes a great deal of difficulty in the minds of many honest inquirers after this truth.

Suppose two friends go to see some celebrated building, and return home to describe it. One has seen only the north side, and the other only the south. The first says, "The building was built in such a maimer, and has such and such stories and ornaments." "Oh, no," says the other, interrupting him, "you are altogether mistaken; I saw the building, and it was built in quite a different manner, and its ornaments and stories were so and so." A lively dispute would probably follow upon the truth of the respective descriptions, until the two friends discover that they have been describing different *sides* of the building, and then all is reconciled at once.

I would like to state as clearly as I can what I judge to be the two distinct sides in this matter; and to show how the looking at one without seeing the other will be sure to create wrong impressions and 'views of the truth.

To state it in brief, I would just say that man's part is to trust, and God's part is to work; and it can be seen at a glance how contrastive these two parts are, and yet not necessarily contradictory. I mean this. There is a certain *work* to be accomplished. We are to be delivered from the power of sin, and are to be made perfect in every good work to do the will of God. "Beholding as in a glass the glory of the Lord," we are to be actually "changed into the same image from glory to glory, even as by the Spirit of the Lord." We are to be transformed by the renewing of our minds, that we may prove what is that good and acceptable and perfect will of God. A real work is to be wrought in us and upon us. Besetting sins are to be conquered. Evil habits are to be overcome. Wrong dispositions and feelings are to be rooted out, and holy tempers and emotions are to be begotten. A positive transformation is to take

8

place. So at least the Bible teaches. Now somebody must do this. Either we must do it for ourselves, or another must do it for us. We have most of us tried to do it for ourselves at first, and have grievously failed; then we discover from the Scriptures and from our own experience that it is a work we are utterly unable to do for ourselves, but that the Lord Jesus Christ has- come on purpose to do it, and that He will do it for all who put themselves wholly into His hand, and trust Him to do it. Now, under these circumstances, what is the part of the believer, and what is the part of the Lord? Plainly the believer can do nothing but trust; while the Lord, in whom he trusts, actually does the work entrusted to Him. *Trusting* and *doing* are certainly contrastive things, and often contradictory; but are they contradictory in this case? Manifestly not, because it is two different parties that are concerned. If we should say of one party in a transaction that he trusted his case to another, and yet attended to it himself, we should state a contradiction and an impossibility. But when we say of two parties in a transaction that one trusts the other to do something, and that that other goes to work and does it, we are stating something that is perfectly simple and harmonious. When we say, therefore, that in this higher life man's part is to trust, and that God does the thing entrusted to Him, we do not surely present any very difficult or puzzling problem.

The preacher who is speaking on man's part in the matter cannot speak of anything but surrender and trust, because this is positively all the man can do. We all agree about this. And yet such preachers are constantly criticised as though, in saying this, they had meant to imply there *was* no other part, and that therefore nothing but trusting is done. And the cry goes out that this doctrine of faith does away with all realities, that souls are just told to trust, and that it is the end of it, and they sit down thenceforward in a sort of religious easy-chair, dreaming away a life fruitless of any actual results. All this misapprehension arises, of course, from the fact that either the preacher has neglected to state, or the hearer has failed to hear, the other side of the matter, which is, that when we trust, the Lord works, and that a great deal is done, not by us, but by Him. Actual results are reached by our trusting, because our

Lord undertakes the thing trusted to Him, and accomplishes it. *We* do not do anything, but *He* does it; and it is all the more effectually done because of this. The puzzle as to the preaching of faith disappears entirely as soon as this is clearly seen.

On the other hand, the preacher who dwells on God's side of the question is criticised on a totally different ground. He does not speak of trust, for the Lord's part is not to trust, but to work. The Lord does the thing entrusted to Him. He disciplines and trains the soul by inward exercises and outward providences. He brings to bear all the resources of His wisdom and love upon the refining and purifying of that soul. He makes everything in the life and circumstances of such an one subservient to the one great purpose of making him grow in grace, and of conforming him, day by day and hour by hour, to the image of Christ. He carries him through a process of transformation, longer or shorter, as his peculiar case may require, making actual and experimental the results for which the soul has trusted. We have dared, for instance, according to the command in Romans 6:11, by faith, to reckon ourselves dead unto sin. The Lord makes this a reality, and leads us to victory over self, by the daily and hourly discipline of His providences. Our reckoning is available only because God thus makes it real. And yet the preacher who dwells upon this practical side of the matter, and tells of God's processes for making faith's reckonings experimental realities, is accused of contradicting the preaching of faith altogether, and of declaring only a process of gradual sanctification by works, and of setting before the soul an impossible and hopeless task.

Now, sanctification is both a sudden step of faith, and also a gradual process of works. It is a step as far as we are concerned; it is a process as to God's part. By a step of faith we get into Christ; by a process we are made to grow up unto Him in all things. By a step of faith we put ourselves into the hands of the Divine Potter; by a gradual process He makes us into a vessel unto His own honour, meet for His use, and prepared to every good work.

To illustrate all this—suppose I were to be describing to a person who was entirely ignorant of the subject, the way in which a lump of clay is made into a beautiful vessel. I tell him first the part of the clay in the matter, and all I can say about this is, that the clay is put into the potter's hands, and then lies passive there, submitting itself to all the turnings and overturnings of the potter's hands upon it. There is really nothing else to be said about the clay's part. But could my hearer argue from this that nothing else is done, because I say that this is all the clay can do? If he is an intelligent hearer he will not dream of doing so, but will say, "I understand. This is what the clay must do; but what must the potter do?" "Ah," I answer, "now we come to the important part. The potter takes the clay thus abandoned to his working, and begins to mould and fashion it according to his own will. He kneads and works it; he tears it apart and presses it together again; he wets it and then suffers it to dry. Sometimes he works at it for hours together; sometimes he lays it aside for days, and does not touch it. And then, when by all these processes he has made it perfectly pliable in his hands, he proceeds to make it up it into the vessel he has purposed. He turns it upon the wheel, planes it and smooths it, and dries it in the sun, bakes it in the oven, and finally turns it out of his workshop a vessel to his honour and fit for his use."

Will my hearer be likely now to say that I am contradicting myself, that a little while ago I had said the clay had nothing to do but to lie passive in the potter's hands, and that now I am putting upon it a great work which it is not able to perform, and that to make itself into such a vessel is an impossible and hopeless undertaking? Surely not. For he will see that while before I was speaking of the clay's part in the matter, I am now speaking of the potter's part, and that these two are necessarily contrastive, but not in the least contradictory; and that the clay is not expected to do the potter's work, but only to yield itself up to his working.

Nothing, it seems to me could be clearer than the perfect harmony between these two *apparently* contradictory sorts of teaching on this subject. What *can* be said about man's part in this great work, but that he must continually surrender himself and continually trust?

But when we come to God's side of the question, what is there that may not be said as to the manifold and wonderful ways in which He accomplishes the work entrusted to Him? It is here that the growing comes in. The lump of clay would never grow into a beautiful vessel if it stayed in the clay-pit for thousands of years. But once put into the hands of a skilful potter, and, under his fashioning, it grows rapidly into a vessel to his honour. And so the soul, abandoned to the working of the Heavenly Potter, is changed rapidly from glory to glory into the image of the Lord by His Spirit.

Having, therefore, taken the step of faith by which you have put yourself wholly and absolutely into His hands, you must now expect Him to begin to work. His way of accomplishing that which you have entrusted to Him may be different from your way. But He knows, and you must be satisfied.

I knew a lady who had entered into this life of faith with a great outpouring of the Spirit, and a wonderful flood of light and joy. She supposed, of course, this was a preparation for some great service, and expected to be put forth immediately into the Lord's harvest field. Instead of this, almost at once her husband lost all his money, and she was shut up in her own house, to attend to all sorts of domestic duties, with no time or strength left for any Gospel work at all. She accepted the discipline, and yielded herself up as heartily to sweep, and dust, and hake, and sew, as she would have done to preach, or pray, or write for the Lord. And the result was that through this very training He made her into a vessel "meet for the Master's use, and prepared unto every good work."

Another lady who had entered this life of faith under similar circumstances of wondrous blessing, and who also expected to be sent out to do some great work, was shut up with two peevish invalid children, to nurse, and humour, and amuse them all day long. Unlike the first lady, this one did not accept the training, but chafed and fretted, and finally rebelled, lost all her blessing, and went back into a state of sad coldness and misery. She had understood her part of trusting to begin with, but not understanding the Divine process of accomplishing that for which she had trusted, she took herself out of the hands of the Heavenly Potter, and the vessel was marred on the wheel.

I believe many a vessel has been similarly marred by a want of understanding these things. The maturity of Christian experience cannot be reached in a moment, but is the result of the work of God's Holy Spirit, who, by His energizing and transforming power, causes us to grow up into Christ in all things. And we cannot hope to reach this maturity in any other way than by yielding ourselves up utterly and willingly to His mighty working. But the sanctification the Scriptures urge as a present experience upon all believers does not consist in maturity of growth, but in purity of heart, and this may be as complete in the babe in Christ as in the veteran believer.

The lump of clay from the moment it comes under the transforming hand of the potter, is, during each day and each hour of the process, just what the potter wants it to be at that hour or on that day, and therefore pleases him. But it is very far from being matured into the vessel he intends in the future to make it.

The little babe may be all that a babe could be, or ought to be, and may therefore perfectly please its mother, and yet it is very far from being what that mother would wish it to be when the years of maturity shall come.

The apple in June is a perfect apple for June. It is the best apple that June can produce. But it is very different from the apple in October, which is a perfected apple.

God's works are perfect in every stage of their growth. Man's works are never perfect until they are in every respect complete.

All that we claim then in this life of sanctification is, that by a step of faith we put ourselves into the hands of the Lord, for Him to work in us all the good pleasure of His will, and that by a continuous exercise of faith we keep ourselves there. This is our part in the matter. And when we do it, and while we do it, we are, in the Scripture sense, truly pleasing to God, although it may require years of training and discipline to mature us into a vessel that shall be in all respects to His honour, and fitted to every good work.

Our part is the trusting, it is His to accomplish the results. And when we do our part He never fails to do His, for no one ever trusted in the Lord and was confounded. Do not be afraid, then, that if you trust or tell others to trust, the matter will end there. Trust is only the beginning and the continual foundation; when we trust, the Lord works, and His work is the important part of the whole matter. And this explains that apparent paradox which puzzles so many. They say, "In one breath you tell us to do nothing but trust, and in the next you tell us to do impossible things. How can you reconcile such contradictory statements?" They are to be reconciled just as we reconcile the statements concerning a saw in a carpenter's shop, when we say at one moment that the saw has sawn asunder a log, and the next moment declare that the carpenter has done it. The saw is the instrument used, the power that uses it is the carpenter's. And so we, yielding ourselves unto God, and our members as instruments of righteousness unto Him, find that He works in us to will and to do of His good pleasure, and we can say with Paul, "I laboured; yet not I, but the grace of God which was with me."

In this book I shall of course dwell mostly upon man's side in the matter, as I am writing for man, and in the hope of teaching believers how to fulfil their part of the great work. But I wish it to be distinctly understood all through, that unless I believed with all my heart in God's effectual working on His side, not one word of this book would ever have been written.

2

THE SCRIPTURALNESS OF THIS LIFE

WHEN I APPROACH subject of the true Christian life,—that life which is hid with Christ in God,—so many thoughts struggle for utterance that I am almost speechless. Where shall I begin? What is the most important thing to say? How shall I make people read and believe? The subject is so glorious, and human words seem so powerless!

But something must be said by some one. The secret must be told. For it is one concerning that victory which overcometh the world,—that promised deliverance from all our enemies, for which every child of God longs and prays, but which seems so often and so generally to elude their grasp. May God grant me so to tell it, that every believer to whom this hook shall come may have his eyes opened to see the truth as it is in Jesus, and may be enabled to enter into possession of this glorious life for himself!

For sure I am, that every converted soul longs for victory and rest, and nearly every one feels instinctively, at times, that they are his birthright. Can you not remember, some of you, the shout of triumph your souls gave when you first became acquainted with the Lord Jesus, and had a glimpse of His mighty saving power? How sure you were of victory, then! How easy it seemed to be more than conquerors, through Him that loved you! Under the leadership of a Captain who had never been foiled in battle, how could you dream of defeat? And yet, to many of you, how different has been your real experience! The victories have been too few and fleeting, the defeats many and disastrous. You have not lived as you feel children of God ought to live. There has been a resting in a clear understanding of doctrinal truth, without pressing after the power and life thereof. There has been a rejoicing in the knowledge of things testified of in the Scriptures, without a living realisation of the things themselves, consciously felt in the soul. Christ is believed in, talked about, and served, but He is not known as the soul's actual and very life, abiding there for ever, and revealing Himself there continually in His beauty. You have found Jesus as your Saviour from the penalty of sin, and you have tried to serve God, and advance the cause of His kingdom. You have carefully studied the Holy Scriptures and have. gathered much precious truth therefrom, which you have endeavoured faithfully to practise. But notwithstanding all your knowledge and all your activities in the service of the Lord, your souls are secretly starving, and you cry out again and again for that bread and water of life which you see promised in the Scriptures to all believers. In the very depths of your hearts, you know that your experience is not a Scriptural experience; that, as an old writer says, your religion is "but a *talk* to what the early Christians enjoyed, possessed, and lived in." And your souls have sunk within you as, day after day, and year after year, your early visions of triumph have seemed to grow more and more dim, and you have been forced to settle down to the conviction, that the best you can expect from your religion is a life of alternate failure and victory; one hour sinning, and the next repenting, and beginning again, only to fail again, and again to repent.

But *is* this all? Had the Lord Jesus only this in His mind when He laid down His precious life to deliver you from your sore and cruel bondage to Satan? Did He propose to Himself only this partial deliverance? Did He intend to leave you thus struggling along under a weary consciousness of defeat and discouragement? Did He fear that a continuous victory would dishonour Him, and bring reproach on His name? When all those declarations were made concerning His coming, and the work He was to accomplish, did they mean only this that you have experienced? Was there a hidden reserve in each promise that was meant to deprive it of its complete fulfilment? Did "delivering us out of the hand of our enemies" mean from only a few of them? Did "enabling us always to triumph" mean only sometimes; or being "more than conquerors through Him that loved us" mean constant defeat and failure? No, No, a thousand times No! God is able to save us to the uttermost, and He meant to do it. His promise, confirmed by His oath, was, that "He would grant unto us, that we, being delivered out of the hand of our enemies, might serve Him without fear, in holiness and righteousness before Him, all the days of our life." It is a mighty work to do, but our Deliverer is able to do it. He came to destroy the works of the devil, and dare we dream for a moment that He is not able or not willing to accomplish His own purposes?

In the very outset, then, settle down on this one thing; that Jesus came to save you fully, now, in this life, from the power and dominion of sin, and to deliver you altogether out of the hands of your enemies. If you do not think He did, search your Bibles, and collect together every announcement or declaration concerning the purposes and object of His death on the cross. You will be astonished to find how full they are. Everywhere and always His work is said to be to deliver us from our sins, from our bondage, from our defilement; and not a hint is given, anywhere, that this deliverance was to be only the limited and partial one with which the Church so continually tries to be satisfied.

Let me give you a few texts on this subject. When the angel of the Lord appeared unto Joseph in a dream, and announced the coming birth of the Saviour, he said "and thou shalt call His name Jesus, for He shall save His people from their sins."

When Zacharias was "filled with the Holy Ghost" at the birth of his son, and "prophesied," he declared that God had visited His people in order to fulfil the promise and the oath He had made them, which promise was, "That He would grant unto us, that we, being delivered out of the hand of our enemies, might serve Him without fear, in holiness and righteousness before Him, all the days of our life."

When Peter was preaching in the porch of the Temple to the wondering Jews, he said, "Unto you first, God, having raised up His Son Jesus, sent Him to bless you in turning away every one of you from his iniquities."

When Paul was telling out to the Ephesian Church the wondrous truth that Christ had loved them so much as to give Himself for them, he went on to declare, that His purpose in thus doing was "that He might sanctify and cleanse it by the washing of water by the word, that He might present it to Himself a glorious Church, not having spot or wrinkle, or any such thing: but that it should be holy and without blemish."

When Paul was seeking to instruct Titus, his own son after the common faith, concerning the grace of God, he declared that the object of that grace was to teach us "that denying ungodliness and worldly lusts, we should live soberly, righteously, and godly in this present world;" and adds, as the reason of this, that Christ "gave Himself for us that He might redeem *us* from all iniquity, and purify us unto Himself a peculiar people, zealous of good works."

When Peter was urging upon the Christians to whom he was writing a holy and Christ-like walk, he tells them that "even. hereunto were ye called because Christ also suffered for us, leaving us an example that ye should follow His steps: who did no sin, neither was guile found in His mouth;" and adds, "who His own self hare our sins in His own body on the tree, that we, being dead to sins, should live unto righteousness; by whose stripes ye were healed."

When Paul was contrasting in the Ephesians the walk suitable for a Christian, with the walk of an unbeliever, he sets before them the truth in Jesus as being this—"that ye put off concerning the former conversation the old man, which is corrupt according to the deceitful lusts; and be renewed in the spirit of your mind; and that ye put on the new man, which after God is created in righteousness and true holiness."

And when, in Romans 6, he was answering for ever the question as to continuing in sin, and showing how utterly foreign it was to the whole spirit and aim of the salvation of Jesus, he brings up the fact of our judicial death and resurrection with Christ as an unanswerable argument for our practical deliverance from it, and says "God forbid. How shall we, that are dead to sin, live any longer therein? Know ye not that so many of us as were baptized into Jesus Christ were baptized into His death? Therefore we are buried with Him by baptism into death; that

18

like as Christ was raised up from the dead by the glory of the Father, even so we also should walk in newness of life." And adds, "knowing this, that our old man is crucified with Him, that the body of sin might be destroyed, that henceforth we should not serve sin."

Dear Christians, will you receive the testimony of Scripture on this matter? The same questions that troubled the Church in Paul's day are troubling it now: first, "Shall we continue in sin that grace may abound?" And second, "Do we then make void the law through faith?" Shall not our answer to these be Paul's emphatic "God forbid," and his triumphant assertions that instead of making it void "we establish the law;" and that "what the law could not do, in that it was weak through the flesh, God sending His own Son in the likeness of sinful flesh, and for sin, condemned sin in the flesh: that the righteousness of the law might be fulfilled in us who walk not after the flesh but after the Spirit?"

Can we suppose for a moment that the holy God, who hates sin in the sinner, is willing to tolerate it in the Christian, and that He has even arranged the plan of salvation in such a way as to make it impossible for those who are saved from the guilt of sin, to find deliverance from its power?

As Dr. Chalmers well says, "Sin is that scandal, which must be rooted out from the great spiritual household over which the Divinity rejoices. . . . Strange administration, indeed, for sin to be so hateful to God, as to lay all who had incurred it under death, and yet when readmitted into life, that sin should be permitted and that what was before the object of destroying vengeance, should now become the object of an upheld and protected toleration. Now that the penalty is taken off, think you it is possible that the unchangeable God has so given up His antipathy to sin, as that man—ruined and redeemed man—may now perseveringly indulge under the new arrangement in that which under the old destroyed him? Does not the God who loved righteousness and hated iniquity six thousand years ago, bear the same love to righteousness and hatred to iniquity still? . . . I now breathe the air of loving-kindness from Heaven, and can walk before God in peace and graciousness; shall I again attempt the incompatible alliance of two principles so adverse as that of an approving God and a persevering sinner? How shall we, recovered from so awful a catastrophe, continue that which first involved us in it? The cross of Christ, by the same mighty and decisive stroke wherewith it moved the curse of sin away from us, also surely moves away the power and the love of it from over us."

And not Dr. Chalmers only, but many other holy men of his generation and of our own, as well as of generations long past, have united in declaring that the redemption accomplished for us by our Lord Jesus Christ on the cross at Calvary, is a redemption from the power of sin as well as from its guilt, and that He *is* able to save to the uttermost all who come unto God by Him.

A quaint old divine of the seventeenth century says: "There is nothing so contrary to God as sin, and Clod will not suffer sin always to rule His masterpiece, man. When we consider the infiniteness of God's power for destroying that which is contrary to Him, who can believe that the devil must always stand and prevail? I believe it is inconsistent and disagreeable with true faith for people to be Christians, and yet to believe that Christ, the eternal Son of God, to whom all power in heaven and earth is given, will suffer sin and the devil to have dominion over them.

"But you will say no man by all the power he hath can redeem himself, and no man can live without sin. We will say Amen to it. But if men tell us that, when God's power comes to help us and to redeem us out of sin, that it cannot be effected, then this doctrine we cannot away with; nor I hope you neither.

"Would you approve of it if I should tell you that God puts forth His power to do such a thing, but the devil hinders Him? That it is impossible for God to do it because the devil does not like it? That it is impossible that any one should be free from sin because the devil hath got such a power in them that God cannot cast him out? This is lamentable doctrine, yet hath not this been preached? It doth in plain terms say, though God doth interpose His power, it is impossible, because the devil hath so rooted sin in the nature of man. Is not man

God's creature, and cannot He new make him, and cast sin out of him? If you say sin is deeply rooted in man, I say so, too; yet not so deeply rooted but Christ Jesus hath entered so deeply into the root of the nature of man that He hath received power to destroy the devil and his works, and to recover and redeem man into righteousness and holiness. Or else it is false that 'He is able to save to the uttermost all that come unto God by Him.' We must throw away the Bible if we say that it is impossible for God to deliver man out of sin.

"We know," he continues, "when our friends are in captivity, as in Turkey, or elsewhere, we pay our money for their redemption; but we will not pay our money if they be kept in their fetters still. Would not any one think himself cheated to pay so much money for their redemption, and the bargain be made so that he shall be *said* to be redeemed, and be *called* a redeemed captive, but he must wear his fetters still? How long? As long as he hath a day to live.

"This is for bodies, but now I am speaking of souls. Christ must be made to me redemption, and rescue me from captivity. Am I a prisoner anywhere? Yes, verily, verily, he that committeth sin, saith Christ, he is a servant of sin, he is a slave of sin. If thou hast sinned, thou art a slave, a captive that must be redeemed out of captivity. Who will pay a price for me? I am poor; I have nothing; I cannot redeem myself; who will pay a price for me? There is One come who hath paid a price for me. That is well; that is good news, then I hope I shall come out of my captivity. What is His name, is He called a Redeemer? So, then, I do expect the benefit of my redemption, and that I shall go out of my captivity. No say they, you must abide in sin as long as you live. What! must we never be delivered? Must this crooked heart and perverse will always remain? Must I be a believer and yet have no faith that reacheth to sanctification and holy living? Is there no mastery to he had, no getting victory over sin? Must it prevail over me as long as I live? What sort of a Redeemer, then, is this, or what benefit have I in this life, of my redemption?"

Similar extracts might be quoted from Marshall, Romaine, and many others, to show that this doctrine is no new one in the Church, however much it may have been lost sight of by the present generation of believers. It is the same old story that has filled with songs of triumph the daily lives of many saints of God throughout all ages; and it is now afresh being sounded forth to the unspeakable joy of weary and burdened souls.

Do not reject it, then, dear reader, until you have prayerfully searched the Scriptures to see whether these things be indeed so. Ask God to open the eyes of your understanding by His Spirit, that you may "know what is the exceeding greatness of His power to usward who believe, according to the working of His mighty power, which He wrought in Christ, when He raised Him from the dead, and set Him at His own right hand in the heavenly places." And when you have begun to have some faint glimpses of this power, learn to look away utterly from your own weakness, and, putting your case into His hands, trust Him to deliver you.

"When thou goest out to battle against thine enemies, and seest horses, and chariots, and a people more than thou, be not afraid of them: for the Lord thy God is with thee, which brought thee up out of the land of Egypt. And it shall be when ye are come nigh unto the battle, that the priest shall approach, and speak unto the people, and shall say unto them, Hear, oh Israel; ye approach this day unto battle against your enemies: let not your hearts faint; fear not and do not tremble, neither be ye terrified because of them; for the Lord your God is He that goeth with you to fight for you against your enemies, to save you."

3

THE LIFE DEFINED

I N MY LAST CHAPTER I tried to settle the question as to the Scripturalness of the experience sometimes called the Higher Christian Life, but which to my own mind is best described in the words, the "life bid with Christ in God." I shall now, therefore, consider it as a settled point that the Scriptures do set before the believer in the Lord Jesus a life of abiding rest and of continual victory, which is very far beyond the ordinary line of Christian experience; and that in the Bible we have presented to us a Saviour able to save us from the power of our sins, as really as He saves us from their guilt.

The point to be next considered is as to what this hidden life consists in, and how it differs from every other sort of Christian experience.

And as to this—it is simply letting the Lord carry our burdens and manage our affairs for us, instead of trying to do it ourselves.

Most Christians are like a man who was toiling along the road, bending under a heavy burden, when a waggon overtook him, and the driver kindly offered to help him on his journey. He joyfully accepted the offer, but when seated continued to bend beneath his burden, which he still kept on his shoulders. "Why do you not lay down your burden?" asked the kindhearted driver. "Oh!" replied the man, "I feel that it is almost too much to ask you to carry me, and could not think of letting you carry my burden too." And so Christians who have given themselves into the care and keeping of the Lord Jesus, still continue to bend beneath the weight of their burden, and often go weary and heavy-laden throughout the whole length of their journey.

When I speak of burdens, I mean everything that troubles us, whether spiritual or temporal.

I mean first of all ourselves. The greatest burden we have to carry in life is self. The most difficult thing we have to manage is self. Our own daily living, our frames and feelings, our especial weaknesses and temptations, and our peculiar temperaments,—our inward affairs of every kind,—these are the things that perplex and worry us more than anything else, and that bring us oftenest into bondage and darkness. In laying off your burdens, therefore, the first one you must get rid of is yourself. You must hand yourself and all your inward experience, your temptations, your temperament, your frames and feelings, all over into the care and keeping of your God, and leave them there. He made you and therefore He understands you and knows how to manage you, and you must trust Him to do it. Say to Him, "Here Lord, I abandon myself to Thee. I have tried in every way I could think of to manage myself, and to make myself what I know I ought to be, but have always failed. Know I give it up to Thee. Do Thou take entire possession of me. Work in me all the good pleasure of Thy will. Mould and fashion me into such a vessel as seemeth good to Thee. I leave myself in Thy hands, and I believe Thou wilt, according to Thy promise, make me into a vessel unto Thine honour, 'sanctified, and meet for the Master's use, and prepared unto every good work.'" And here you must rest, trusting yourself thus to Him continually and absolutely.

Next, you must lay off every other burden: your health, your reputation, your Christian work, your houses, your children, your business, your servants,—everything, in short, that concerns you, whether inward or outward.

Christians always commit the keeping of their souls for eternity to the Lord, because they know, without a shadow of a doubt, that they cannot keep themselves. But the things of this present life they take into their own keeping, and try to carry on their own shoulders, with the perhaps unconfessed feeling that it is a great deal to ask the Lord to carry them, and that they cannot think of asking Him to carry their burdens too.

I knew a Christian lady who had a very heavy temporal burden. It took away her sleep and her appetite, and there was danger of her health breaking down under it. One day, when it seemed especially heavy, she noticed lying on the table near her a little tract called "Hannah's Faith."

Attracted by the title, she picked it up and began to read it, little knowing, however, that it was to create a revolution in her whole experience. The story was of a poor woman who had been carried triumphantly through a life of unusual sorrow. She was giving the history of her life to a kind visitor on one occasion, and at the close the visitor said, feelingly, "Oh, Hannah, I do not see how you could bear so much sorrow!" "I did not bear it," was the quick reply; "the Lord bore it for me." "Yes," said the visitor, "that is the right way. You must take your troubles to the Lord." "Yes," replied Hannah, "but we must do more than that: we must *leave* them there. Most people," she continued, "take their burdens to Him, but they bring them away with them again, and are just as worried and unhappy as ever. But I take mine, and I leave them with Him, and come away and forget them. And if the worry comes back, I take it to Him again; I do this over and over, until at last I just forget that I have any worries, and am at perfect rest."

My friend was very much struck with this plan, and resolved to try it. The circumstances of her life she could not alter, but she took them to the Lord, and handed them over into His management; and then she believed that He took it, and she left all the responsibility, and the worry and anxiety, with Him. As often as the anxieties returned she took them back; and the result was that, although the circumstances remained unchanged, her soul was kept in perfect peace in the midst of them. She felt that she had found out a blessed secret, and from that time she never again tried to carry her own burdens, nor to manage anything for herself.

And the secret she found so effectual in her outward affairs she found to be still more effectual in her inward ones, which were in truth even more utterly unmanageable. She abandoned her whole self to the Lord, with all that she was and all that she had, and, believing that He took that which she had committed to Him, she ceased to fret and worry, and her life became all sunshine in the gladness of belonging to Him. And this was "the Higher Christian Life"! It was a very simple secret she found out—only this: that it was possible to obey God's commandment contained in those words, "Be careful for nothing; but in

25

everything by prayer and supplication, with thanksgiving, let your requests be made known unto God;" and that, in obeying it, the result would inevitably be, according to the promise, that the "peace of God which passeth all understanding shall keep your hearts and minds through Christ Jesus."

There are many other things to be said about this life hid with Christ in God, many details as to what the Lord Jesus does for those who thus abandon themselves to Him. But the gist of the whole matter is here stated, and the soul that has got hold of this secret has found the key that will unlock the whole treasure-house of God.

And now I do trust that I have made you hungry for this blessed life. Would you not like to get rid of your burdens? Do you not long to hand over the management of your unmanageable self into the hands of One who is able to manage you? Are you not tired and weary, and does not the rest I speak of look sweet to you? Do you recollect the delicious sense of rest with which you have sometimes gone to bed at night, after a day of great exertion and weariness? How delightful was the sensation of relaxing every muscle, and letting your body go in a perfect abandonment of ease and comfort. The strain of the day had ceased for a few hours at least, and the work of the day had been laid off. You no longer had to hold up an aching head or a weary back. You trusted yourself to the bed in an absolute confidence, and it held you up, without effort, or strain, or even thought on your part. You rested!

But suppose you had doubted the strength or the stability of your bed, and had dreaded each moment to find it giving way beneath you and landing you on the floor; could you have rested then? Would not every muscle have been strained in a fruitless effort to hold yourself up, and would not the weariness have been greater than not to have gone to bed at all?

Let this analogy teach you what it means to rest in the Lord. Let your souls lie down upon His sweet will, as your bodies lie down in your beds at night. Relax every strain and lay off every burden. Let yourself go in a perfect abandonment of ease and comfort, sure that when He holds you up you are perfectly safe.

Your part is simply to rest. His part is to sustain you, and He cannot fail.

Or take another analogy, which our Lord Himself has abundantly sanctioned—that of the child-life. For "Jesus called a little child unto Him, and set him in the midst of them, and said, Verily I say unto you, Except ye be converted, and become as little children, ye shall not enter into the kingdom of heaven."

Now, what are the characteristics of a little child, and how does he live? He lives by faith, and his chiefest characteristic is thoughtlessness. His life is one long trust from year's end to year's end. He trusts his parents, he trusts his care-takers, he trusts his teachers, he even trusts people often who are utterly unworthy of trust, because of the confidingness of his nature. And his trust is abundantly answered. He provides nothing for himself, and yet everything is provided. He takes no thought for the morrow, and forms no plans, and yet all his life is planned out for him, and he finds his paths made ready, opening out to him as he comes to them day by day and hour by hour. He goes in and out of his father's house with an unspeakable ease and abandonment, enjoying all the good things it contains, without having spent a penny in procuring them. Pestilence may walk through the streets of his city, but he regards it not. Famine and fire and war may rage around him, but under his father's tender care he abides in utter unconcern and perfect rest. He lives in the present moment, and receives his life without question as it comes to him day by day from his father's hands.

I was visiting once in a wealthy house, where there was one only adopted child, upon whom was lavished all the love and tenderness and care that human hearts could bestow, or human means procure. And as I watched that child running in and out day by day, free and light-hearted, with the happy carelessness of childhood, I thought what a picture it was of our wonderful position as children in the house of our Heavenly Father. And I said to myself, If nothing could so grieve and wound the loving hearts around her, as to see this little child beginning to be worried or anxious about herself in any way,—about whether her food and clothes would be provided for her, or how she was to get her education or her future support,—how much more must the great, loving heart of our God and Father be grieved and wounded at seeing His children taking so much anxious care and thought! And I understood why it was that our Lord had said to us so emphatically, "Take no thought for yourselves."

"Who is the best cared for in every household? Is it not the little children? And does not the least of all, the helpless baby, receive the largest share? As a late writer has said, the baby "toils not, neither does he spin; and yet he is fed, and clothed, and loved, and rejoiced in," and none so much as he.

This life of faith, then, about which I am writing, consists in just this—being a child in the Father's house. And when this is said, enough is said to transform every weary, burdened life into one of blessedness and rest.

Let the ways of childish confidence and freedom from care which so please you and win your hearts in your own little ones, teach you what should be your ways with God; and leaving yourselves in His hands, learn to be literally careful for nothing; and you shall find it to be a fact that "the peace of God which passeth all understanding shall keep (as in a garrison) your hearts and minds through Christ Jesus."

"Trust in the Lord and do good: so shalt thou dwell in the land, and verily thou shalt be fed.

"Delight thyself also in the Lord; and He shall give thee the desires of thine heart.

"Commit thy way unto the Lord; trust also in Him, and He shall bring it to pass:

"And He shall bring forth thy righteousness as the light, and thy judgment as the noon-day.

"Rest in the Lord, and wait patiently for Him."

"And the work of righteousness shall be peace; and the effect of righteousness, quietness and assurance for ever.

"And my people shall dwell in a peaceable habitation, and in sure dwellings, and in quiet resting-places."

4

HOW TO ENTER IN

AVING TRIED TO SETTLE the question as to the
Scripturalness of the experience of this life of full trust, and
having also shown a little of what it is, the next point is as to
how it is to be reached and realized.

And first I would say that this blessed life must not be looked upon
in any sense as an attainment but as an obtainment. We cannot earn it,
we cannot climb up to it, we cannot win it; we can do nothing but ask
for it and receive it. It is the gift of God in Christ Jesus. And where a
thing is a gift, the only course left for the receiver is to take it and thank
the giver. We never say of a gift, "See to what I have attained," and
boast of our skill and wisdom in having attained it; but we say, "See
what has been given me," and boast of the love, and wealth, and
generosity of the giver. And everything in our salvation is a gift. From
beginning to end God is the giver and we are the receivers; and it is not
to those who do great things, but to those who "receive abundance of
grace, and of the gift of righteousness," that the richest promises are
made. In order, therefore, to enter, into a realized experience of this
interior life, the soul must be in a receptive attitude, fully recognizing the
fact that it is to be God's gift in Christ Jesus, and that it cannot be
gained by any efforts or works of our own. This will simplify the matter
exceedingly, and the only thing left to he considered then will be to
discover upon whom God bestows this gift, and how they are to receive
it. And to this I would answer in short, that He bestows it only upon the
fully consecrated soul, and that it is to be received by faith.

Consecration is the first thing. Not in any legal sense, not in order
to purchase or deserve the blessing, but to remove the difficulties out of
the way and make it possible for God to bestow it. In order for a lump
of clay to be made into a beautiful vessel it must be entirely abandoned
to the potter, and must lie passive in his hands. And in order for a soul

to be made into a vessel unto God's honour, "sanctified and meet for the Master's use, and prepared unto every good work," it must be entirely abandoned to Him, and must lie passive in His hands. This is manifest at the first glance.

I was once trying to explain to a physician who had charge of a large hospital, what consecration meant, and its necessity, but he seemed unable to understand. At last I said to him, "Suppose, in going your rounds among your patients, you should meet with one man who entreated you earnestly to take his case under your especial care in order to cure him, but who should at the same time refuse to tell you all the symptoms, or to take all your prescribed remedies; and should say to you, 'I am quite willing to follow your directions as to certain things, because they commend themselves to my mind as good, but in other matters I prefer judging for myself and following my own directions.' What would you do in such a case," I asked. "Do!" he replied with indignation, "Do! I would soon leave such a man as that to his own care. For of course," he added, "I could do nothing for him, unless he would put his whole case into my hands without any reserves, and would obey my directions implicitly." "It is necessary then," I said, "for doctors to be obeyed, if they are to have any chance to cure their patients?" *"Implicitly obeyed!"* was his emphatic reply. "And that is consecration," I continued. "God must have the whole case put into His hands without any reserves, and His directions must be implicitly followed." "I see it," he exclaimed, "I see it! And I will do it. God shall have His own way with me from henceforth."

Perhaps to some minds the word abandonment might express this idea better. But whatever word we use, we mean an entire surrender of the whole being to God—spirit, soul, and body placed under His absolute control, for Him to do with us just what He pleases. We mean that the language of our souls under all circumstances, and in view of every act, is to be "Thy will be done." We mean the giving up of all liberty of choice. We mean a life of inevitable obedience.

To a soul ignorant of God this may look hard. But to those who know Him, it is the happiest and most restful of lives. He is our Father, and He loves us, and He knows just what is best, and therefore, of course, His will is the very most blessed thing that can come to us under all circumstances. I do not understand how it is that Satan has succeeded in blinding the eyes of the Church to this fact. But it really would seem as if God's own children were more afraid of His will than of anything else in life—His lovely, loveable will, which only means loving kindnesses and tender mercies, and blessings unspeakable to their souls! I wish I could only show to every one the unfathomable sweetness of the will of God. Heaven is a place of infinite bliss because His will is perfectly done there, and our lives share in this bliss just in proportion as His will is perfectly done in them. He loves us—*loves us*—and the will of love is always blessing for its loved one. Some of us know what it is to love, and we know that could we only have our way, our beloved ones would be overwhelmed with blessings. All that is good, and sweet, and lovely in life would be poured out upon them from our lavish hands, had we but the power to carry out our will for them. And if this is the way of love with us, how much more must it be so with our God who is Love itself. Could we but for one moment get a glimpse into the mighty depths of His love, our hearts would spring out to meet His will, and embrace it as our richest treasure. And we would abandon ourselves to it with an enthusiasm of gratitude and joy, that such a wondrous privilege could be ours.

A great many Christians actually seem to think that all their Father in heaven wants is a chance to make them miserable, and to take away all their blessings; and they imagine, poor souls, that if they hold on to things in their own will they can hinder Him from doing this. I am ashamed to write the words, and yet we must face a fact which is making wretched hundreds of lives.

A Christian lady who had this feeling, was once expressing to a friend how impossible she found it to say, "Thy will be done," and how afraid she should be to do it. She was the mother of one only little boy, who was the heir to a great fortune, and the idol of her heart. After she had stated her difficulties fully, her friend said, "Suppose your little Charley should come running to you to-morrow and say 'Mother, I have made up my mind to let you have your own way with me from this time forward. I am always going to obey you, and I want you to do just whatever you think best with me. I know you love me, and I am going to trust myself to your love.' How would you feel towards him? Would you say to yourself, 'Ah, now I shall have a chance to make Charley miserable. I will take away all his pleasures, and nil his life with every hard and disagreeable thing I can find. I will compel him to do just the things that are the most difficult for him to do, and will give him all sorts of impossible commands." "Oh, no, no, no!" exclaimed the indignant mother. "You know I would not. You know I would hug him to my heart and cover him with kisses, and would hasten to fill his life with all that was sweetest and best." "And are you more tender and more loving than God?" asked her friend. "Ah, no," was the reply, "I see my mistake, and I will not be any more afraid of saying, 'Thy will be done,' to my Heavenly Father, than I would want my Charley to be of saying it to me."

Better and sweeter than health, or friends, or money, or fame, or ease, or prosperity, is the adorable will of our God. It gilds the darkest hours with a divine halo, and sheds brightest sunshine on the gloomiest paths. Ho always reigns who has made it His kingdom; and nothing can go amiss to him. Surely, then, it is nothing but a glorious privilege that is opening before you when I tell you that the first step you must take in order to enter into the life hid with Christ in God is that of entire consecration. I cannot have you look at it as a hard and stern demand. You must do it gladly, thankfully, enthusiastically. You must go in on what I call the privilege side of consecration; and I can assure you, from a blessed experience, that you will find it the happiest place you have ever entered yet.

Faith is the next thing. Faith is an absolutely necessary element in the reception of any gift; for let our friends give a thing to us ever so fully, it is not really ours until we believe it has been given, and claim it as our own. Above all, this is true in gifts which are purely mental or spiritual. Love may be lavished upon us by another without stint or measure, but until we believe that we are loved, it never really becomes ours. I suppose most Christians understand this principle in reference to the matter of their forgiveness. They know that the forgiveness of sins through Jesus might have been preached to them forever, but it would never really have become theirs until they believed this preaching, and claimed the forgiveness as their own. But when it comes to living the Christian life, they lose sight of this principle, and think that, having been saved by faith, they are now to live by works and efforts; and instead of continuing to *receive,* they are now to begin to *do.* This makes our declaration that the life hid with Christ in God is to be entered by faith, seem perfectly unintelligible to them. And yet it is plainly declared, that *"as* we have received Christ Jesus the Lord *so* we are to walk in Him." We received Him by faith, and by faith alone; therefore we are to walk in Him by faith, and by faith alone. And the faith by which we enter into this hidden life is just the same as the faith by which we were translated out of the kingdom of Satan into the kingdom of God's dear Son, only it lays hold of a different thing. Then we believed that Jesus was our Saviour from the guilt of sin, and according to our faith it was unto us. Now we must believe that Ho is our Saviour from the power of sin, and according to our faith it shall be unto us. Then we trusted Him for our justification and it became ours; now we must trust Him for our sanctification, and it shall become ours also. Then we took Him as a Saviour in the future from the penalties of our sins; now we must take Him as a Saviour in the present from the bondage of our sins. Then He was our Substitute, now He is to be our Life. Then He lifted us out of the pit, now He is to seat us in heavenly places with Himself.

I mean all this of course experimentally and practically. Theologically and judicially I know that every believer has everything the minute he is converted. But experimentally nothing is his until by faith he claims it. "Every place that the sole of your foot shall tread upon, that have I given unto you." God "hath blessed us with all spiritual blessings in heavenly places in Christ," but until we set the foot of faith upon them they do not practically become ours. "According to our faith," is always the limit and the rule.

But this faith of which I am speaking must be a present faith. No faith that is exercised in the future tense amounts to anything. A man may believe forever that his sins will be forgiven at some future time, and he will never be converted. He has to come to the *now* belief, and say by faith, "My sins are now forgiven," before he can know the new birth. And, similarly, no faith which looks for a future deliverance from the power of sin will ever lead a soul into the life we are describing. Satan delights in this future faith, for he knows it is powerless to accomplish any practical results. But he trembles and flees when the soul of the believer dares to claim a present deliverance, and to reckon itself now to be free from his power.

To sum up, then. In order to enter into this blessed interior life of rest and triumph you have two steps to take. First, entire abandonment; and, second, absolute faith. No matter what may be the complications of your peculiar experience, no matter what your difficulties, or your surroundings, or your associations, these two steps, definitely taken and unwaveringly persevered in, will certainly bring you out sooner or later into the green pastures and still waters of this higher Christian life. You may be sure of this. And if you will let every other consideration go, and simply devote your attention to these two points, and be very clear and definite about them, your progress will be rapid, and your soul will reach its desired haven far sooner than now you can think possible.

Shall I repeat the steps that there may be no mistake? You are a child of God, and long to please Him. You love your precious Saviour, and are sick and weary of the sin that grieves Him. You long to be delivered from its power. Everything you have hitherto tried has failed to deliver you; and now in your despair you are asking if it can indeed be, as these happy people say, that Jesus is able and willing to deliver you. Surely you know in your very soul that He is. That to save you out of the hand of all your enemies is in fact just the very thing He came to do. Then trust Him. Commit your case to Him in an absolute abandonment, and believe that He undertakes it: and at once, knowing what He is and what He has said, claim that He does even now fully save. Just as you believed at first that He delivered you from the guilt of sin because He said so, so now believe that He delivers you from the power of sin because He says so. Lot your faith now lay hold of a new power in Christ. You have trusted Him as your dying Saviour, now trust Him as your living Saviour. Just as much as He came to deliver you from future punishment did He also come to deliver you from present bondage. Just as truly as He came to bear your stripes for you, has He come to live your life for you. You are as utterly powerless in the one case as in the other. You could as easily have got yourself rid of your own sins, as you could now accomplish for yourself practical righteousness. Christ, and Christ only, must do both for you, and your part in both cases is simply to give the thing to Him to do, and then believe that He does it.

A lady, now very eminent in this life of trust, when she was seeking in great darkness and perplexity to enter in, said to the friend who was trying to help her, "You all say abandon yourself and trust—abandon yourself and trust—but I do not know how. I wish you would just do it out loud so that I may see how you do it."

Shall I do it out loud for you?

"Lord Jesus; I believe that Thou art able and willing to deliver me from all the care, and unrest, and bondage of my Christian life. I believe Thou didst die to set me free, not only in the future, but now and here. I believe Thou art stronger than Satan, and that Thou canst keep me, even me, in my extreme of weakness, from falling into his snares, or yielding obedience to his commands. And, Lord, I am going to trust Thee to keep me. I have tried keeping myself, and have foiled, and failed most grievously. I am absolutely helpless. So now I will trust Thee. I give myself to Thee. I keep back no reserves. Body, soul, and spirit, I present myself to Thee, a worthless lump of clay, to be made into anything Thy love and Thy wisdom shall choose. And now, I *am* Thine. I believe Thou dost accept that which I present to Thee; I believe that this poor, weak foolish heart has been taken possession of by Thee, and that Thou hast even at this very moment begun to work in me to will and to do of Thy good pleasure. I trust Thee utterly, and I trust Thee now!"

Are you afraid to take this step? Does it seem too sudden, too much like a leap in the dark? Do you not know that the steps of faith always "fall on the coming void, but find the rock beneath?" If ever you are to enter this glorious land, flowing with milk and honey, you must sooner or later step into the brimming waters, for there is no other path. And to do it now, may save you months and even years of disappointment and grief. Hear the word of the Lord,—

"Have not I commanded thee? Be strong and of a good courage; be not afraid, neither be thou dismayed: for the Lord thy God is with thee withersoever thou goest."

5

DIFFICULTIES CONCERNING CONSECRATION

I T IS VERY IMPORTANT that Christians should not be ignorant of the devices of Satan; for he stands ready to oppose every onward step of the soul's progress. And especially is he busy when he sees a believer awakened to a hunger and thirst after righteousness, and seeking to reach out to apprehend all the fulness that is in the Lord Jesus Christ for him.

One of the first difficulties he throws in the way of such a one is concerning consecration. The seeker after holiness is told that he must consecrate himself, and he endeavours to do so. But at once he meets with a difficulty. He has done it, as he thinks, and *yet* does not feel differently from before; nothing seems changed, as he has been led to expect it would be, and he is completely baffled, and asks the question almost despairingly, "How am I to know when I am consecrated?"

The one grand device of Satan which has met such a soul at this juncture is one which he never fails to employ on every possible occasion, and generally with marked success, and that is in reference to feeling. The soul cannot believe it is consecrated until it feels that it is; and because it does not feel that God has taken it in hand, it cannot believe that He has. As usual, it puts feeling first and faith second. Now, God's invariable rule is faith first and feeling second, in everything; and it is striving against the inevitable when we seek to make it different.

The way to meet this device of Satan, then, in reference to consecration, is simply to take God's side in the matter, and to put faith before feeling. Give yourself to the Lord definitely and fully, according to your present light, asking the Holy Spirit to show you all that is contrary to God, either in your heart or life. If He shows you anything, give it to the Lord immediately, and say in reference to it, "Thy will be done." If He shows you nothing, then you must believe that there is nothing, and must conclude that you have given Him all. Then you must believe that He takes you. You positively must not wait to *feel* either that you have given yourself, or that He has taken you. You must simply believe it, and reckon it to be the case.

If you were to give an estate to a friend, you would have to give it, and he would have to receive it by faith. An estate is not a thing that can be picked up and handed over to another; the gift of it and its reception are altogether a mental transaction, and therefore one of faith. Now, if you should give an estate one day to a friend, and then should go away and wonder whether you really had given it, and whether he actually had taken it and considered it his own, and should feel it necessary to go the next day and renew the gift; and if on the third day you should still feel a similar uncertainty about it, and should again go and renew the gift; and on the fourth day go through a like process, and so on, day after day for months and years, what would your friend think, and what at last would be the condition of your own mind in reference to it? Your friend certainly would begin to doubt whether you ever had intended to give it to him at all, and you yourself would be in such hopeless perplexity about it, that you would not know whether the estate was yours or his, or whose it was.

Now is not this very much the way in which you have been acting towards God in this matter of consecration? You have given yourself to Him over and over, daily perhaps for months, but you have invariably come away from your seasons of consecration wondering whether you really have given yourself after all, and whether He has taken you; and because you have not *felt* any differently, you have concluded at last, after many painful tossings, that the thing has not been done. Do you know, dear believer, that this sort of perplexity will last for ever, unless you cut it short by faith? You must come to the point of reckoning the matter to be an accomplished and settled thing, and leaving it there, before you can possibly expect any change of feeling whatever.

The very law of offerings to the Lord settles this as a primary fact, that everything which is given to Him becomes by that very act something holy, set apart from all other things, and cannot without sacrilege be put to any other uses. "Notwithstanding, no devoted thing that a man shall devote unto the Lord of all that he hath, both of man and beast, and of the field of his possession, shall be sold or redeemed: every devoted thing is most holy unto the Lord." Having once given it to the Lord, the devoted thing henceforth was reckoned by all Israel as being the Lord's, and no one dared to stretch forth a hand to retake it. The giver might have made his offering very grudgingly and halfheartedly, but having made it, the matter was taken out of his hands altogether, and the devoted thing by God's own law became "most holy unto the Lord." It was not the intention of the giver that made it holy, but the holiness of the receiver. "The altar sanctifies the gift." And an offering once laid upon the altar, from that moment belonged to the Lord. I can imagine an offerer who had deposited a gift beginning to search his heart as to his sincerity and honesty in doing it, and coming back to the priest to say that he was afraid after all he had not given it right, or had not been perfectly sincere in giving it. I feel sure that the priest would have silenced him at once with saying, "As to how you gave your offering, or what were your motives in giving it, I do not know. The facts are that you did give it, and that it is the Lord's, for every devoted thing is most holy unto Him. It is too late to recall the transaction now." And not only the priest but all Israel would have been aghast at the man who, having once given his offering, should have reached out his hand to take it back. And yet, day after day, earnest-hearted Christians, who would have shuddered at such an act of sacrilege on the part of a Jew, are guilty in their own experience of a similar act, by giving themselves to the Lord in solemn consecration, and then through unbelief taking back that which they have given.

Because God is not visibly present to the eye, it is difficult to feel that a transaction with Him is real. I suppose if, when we made our acts of consecration, we could actually see Him present with us, we should feel it to be a very real thing, and would realise that we had given our word to Him and could not dare to take it back, no matter how much we might wish to do so. Such a transaction would have to us the binding power that a spoken promise to an earthly friend always has to a man of honour. And what we need is to see that God's presence is a certain fact always, and that every act of our soul is done right before Him, and that a word spoken in prayer is as really spoken to Him as if our eyes could see Him and our hands could touch Him. Then we shall cease to have such vague conceptions of our relations with Him, and shall feel the binding force of every word we say in His presence.

I know some will say here, "Ah, yes; but if He would only speak to me, and say that He took me when I gave myself to Him, I would have no trouble then in believing it." No, of course you would not, but He does not generally say this until the soul has first proved its loyalty by believing what He has already said. It is he that believeth who has the witness, not he that doubteth. And by His very command to us to present ourselves to Him a living sacrifice, He has pledged Himself to receive us. I cannot conceive of an honourable man asking another to give him a thing which, after all, he was doubtful about taking; still less can I conceive of a loving parent acting so towards a darling child. "My son, give me thy heart," is a sure warrant for knowing that the moment the heart is given it will be taken by the One who has commanded the gift. We may, nay we must, feel the utmost confidence then that when we surrender ourselves to the Lord, according to His own command, He does then and there receive us, and from that moment we are His. A real transaction has taken place, which cannot be violated without dishonour on our part, and which we know will not be violated by Him.

In Deut. 26:17, 18, 19, we see God's way of working under these circumstances.

"Thou hast avouched the Lord this day to be thy God, and to walk in His ways and to keep His statutes, and His commandments, and His judgments, and to hearken unto His voice; and the Lord hath avouched thee this day to be His peculiar people, as He hath promised thee, and that thou shouldst keep all His commandments;" . . . "and that thou mayest be an holy people unto the Lord, as He hath spoken."

When we avouch the Lord to be our God, and that we will walk in His ways and keep His commandments, He avouches us to be His, and that we shall keep all His commandments. And from that moment He takes possession of us. This has always been His principle of working, and it continues to be so. "Every devoted thing is most holy to the Lord." This seems to me so plain as scarcely to admit of a question.

But if the soul still feels in doubt or difficulty, let me refer you to a New Testament declaration which approaches the subject from a different side, but which settles it, I think, quite as definitely. It is in 1 John 5:14, 15, and reads, "And this is the confidence that we have in Him, that if we ask anything according to His will, He heareth us; and if we know that He hear us, whatsoever we ask, we know that we *have* the petitions that we desired of Him." Is it according to His will that you should be entirely consecrated to Him? There can be, of course, but one answer to this, for He has *commanded* it. Is it not also according to His will that He should work in you to will and to do of His good pleasure? This question also can have but one answer, for He has declared it to be His purpose. You know, then, that these things are according to His will, therefore on God's own word you are obliged to know that He hears you. And knowing this much, you are compelled to go further, and know that you have the petitions that you have desired of Him. That you *have,* I say, not will have, or may have, but have now in actual possession. It is thus that we "obtain promises" by faith. It is thus that we have "access by faith" into the grace that is given us in our Lord Jesus Christ. It is thus, and thus only, that we come to know our hearts "purified by faith," and are enabled to live by faith, to stand by faith, to walk by faith.

I desire to make this subject so plain and practical that no one need have any further difficulty about it, and therefore I will repeat again just what must be the acts of your soul in order to bring you out of this difficulty about consecration.

I suppose that you have trusted the Lord Jesus for the forgiveness of your sins, and know something of what it is to belong to the family of God, and to be made an heir of God through faith in Christ. And now you feel springing up in your soul the longing to be conformed to the image of your Lord. In order for this you know there must be an entire surrender of yourself to Him, that He may work in you all the good pleasure of His will; and you have tried over and over to do it, but hitherto without any apparent success. At this point it is that I desire to help you. What you must do now is to come once more to Him in a surrender of your whole self to His will, as complete as you know how to make it. You must ask him to reveal to you by His Spirit any hidden rebellion; and if He reveals nothing, then you must believe that there is nothing, and that the surrender is complete. This must, then, be considered a settled matter; you have abandoned yourself to the Lord, and from henceforth you do not in any sense belong to yourself; you must never even so much as listen to a suggestion to the contrary. If the temptation comes to wonder whether you really have completely surrendered yourself, meet it with an assertion that you have. Do not even argue the matter. Repel any such idea instantly, and with decision. You meant it then, you mean it now, you have really done it. Your emotions may clamour against the surrender, but your will must hold firm. It is your purpose God looks at, not your feelings about that purpose; and your purpose, or will, is therefore the only thing you need attend to.

The surrender, then, having been made, never to be questioned or recalled, the next point is to believe that God takes that which you have surrendered, and to reckon that it is His. Not that it will be at some future time, but is now; and that He has begun to work in you to will, and to do, of His good pleasure. And here you must rest. There is nothing more for you to do, for you are the Lord's now, absolutely and entirely in His hands, and He has undertaken the whole care and management and forming of you, and will, according to His word, "work in you that which is well pleasing in His sight through Jesus Christ." But you must hold steadily here. If you begin to question your surrender, or God's acceptance of it, then your wavering faith will produce a wavering experience, and He will not work. But while you trust, He works, and the result of His working always is to change you into the image of Christ, from glory to glory, by His mighty Spirit.

Do you, then, now at this moment surrender yourself wholly to Him? You answer, Yes. Then, my dear friend, begin at once to reckon that you are His; that He has taken you, and that He is working in you to will and to do of His good pleasure. And keep on reckoning this. You will find it a great help to put your reckoning into words, and to say over and over to yourself and to your God, "Lord, I am Thine; I do yield myself up to Thee entirely, and I believe that Thou dost take me. I leave myself with Thee. Work in me all the good pleasure of Thy will, and I will only lie still in Thy hands, and trust Thee." Make this a daily definite act of your will, and many times a day recur to it, as being your continual attitude before Him. Confess it to yourself. Confess it to your God. Confess it to your friends. Avouch the Lord to be your God continually and unwaveringly, and declare your purpose of walking in His ways and keeping His statutes; and you will find in practical experience that He has avouched you to be His peculiar people and that you shall keep all His commandments, and that you will be "an holy people unto the Lord, as He hath spoken."

6

DIFFICULTIES CONCERNING FAITH

THE NEXT STEP AFTER Consecration, in the soul's progress out of the wilderness of Christian experience into the land that floweth with milk and honey, is that of Faith. And here, as in the first step, Satan is very skilful in making difficulties and interposing obstacles.

The child of God, having had his eyes opened to see the fulness there is in Jesus for him, and having been made to long to appropriate that fulness to himself, is met with the assertion on the part of every teacher to whom he applies, that this fulness is only to be received by faith. But the subject of faith is involved in such a hopeless mystery in his mind, that this assertion, instead of throwing light upon the way of entrance, only seems to make it more difficult and involved than ever.

"Of course it is to be by faith," he says, "for I know that everything in the Christian life is by faith. But then that is just what makes it so hard, for I have no faith, and I do not even know what it is, nor how to get it." And, baffled at the very outset by this insuperable difficulty, he is plunged into darkness, and almost despair.

This trouble all arises from the fact that the subject of faith is very generally misunderstood; for in reality faith is the simplest and plainest thing in the world, and the most easy of attainment.

Your idea of faith, I suppose, has been something like this. You have looked upon it as in some way a sort of *thing*, either a religious exercise of soul, or an inward gracious disposition of heart, something tangible, in fact, which, when you have got, you can look at and rejoice over, and use as a passport to God's favour, or a coin with which to purchase His gifts. And you have been praying for faith, expecting all the while to get something like this, and never having received any such thing, you are insisting upon it that you have no faith. Now faith, in fact, is not in the least this sort of a thing. It is nothing at all tangible. It is simply believing God, and, like sight, it is nothing apart from its object. You might as well shut your eyes and look inside, and see whether you have sight, as to look inside to discover whether you have faith. You see something, and thus know that you have sight; you believe something, and thus know that you have faith. For as sight is only seeing, so faith is only believing. And as the only necessary thing about seeing is, that you see the thing as it is, so the only necessary thing about believing is, that you believe the thing as it is. The virtue does not lie in your believing, but in the thing you believe. If you believe the truth you are saved; if you believe a he you are lost. The believing in "both cases is the same; the things believed in are exactly opposite, and it is this which makes the mighty difference. Your salvation comes, not because your faith saves you, but because it links you on to the Saviour who saves; and your believing is really nothing but the link.

I do beg of you to recognise, then, the extreme simplicity of faith, that it is nothing more nor less than just believing God when He says He either has done something for us, or will do it; and then trusting Him to do it. It is so simple that it is hard to explain. If anyone asks me what it means to trust another to do a piece of work for me, I can only answer that it means letting that other one do it, and feeling it perfectly unnecessary for me to do it myself. Every one of us has trusted very important pieces of work to others in this way, and has felt perfect rest in thus trusting, because of the confidence we have had in those who have undertaken to do it. How constantly do mothers trust their most precious infants to the care of nurses, and feel no shadow of anxiety? How continually we are all of us trusting our health and our lives, without a thought of fear, to cooks and coachmen, engine-drivers, railway conductors, and all sorts of paid servants, who have us completely at their mercy, and could plunge us into misery or death in a moment, if they chose to do so, or even if they failed in the necessary carefulness? All this we do, and make no fuss about it. Upon the slightest acquaintance, often, we thus put our trust in people, requiring only the general knowledge of human nature, and the common rules of human intercourse; and we never feel as if we were, doing anything in the least remarkable.

You have done all this yourself, dear reader, and are doing it continually. You would not be able to live in this world and go through the customary routine of life a single day, if you could not trust your fellowmen. And it never enters into your head to say you cannot.

But yet you do not hesitate to say, continually, that you cannot trust your God!

I wish you would just now try to imagine yourself acting in your human relations as you do in your spiritual relations. Suppose you should begin to-morrow with the notion in your head that you could not trust anybody, because you had no faith. "When you sat down to breakfast you would say, "I cannot eat anything on this table, for I have no faith, and I cannot believe the cook has not put poison in the coffee, or that the butcher has not sent home a diseased ham." So you would go starving away. Then when you went out to your daily avocations, you would say, "I cannot ride in the railway train, for I have no faith, and therefore I cannot trust the engineer, nor the conductor, nor the builders of the carriages, nor the managers of the road." So you would be compelled to walk everywhere, and grow unutterably weary in the effort, besides being actually unable to reach many of the places you could have reached in the train. Then when your friends met you with any statements, or your business agent with any accounts, you would say, "I am very sorry that I cannot believe you, but I have no faith, and never can believe anybody." If you opened a newspaper, you would be forced to lay it down again, saying, "I really cannot believe a word this paper says, for I have no faith; I do not believe there is any such person as the Queen, for I never saw her; nor any such country as Ireland, for I was never there. And I have no faith, so of course I cannot believe anything that I have not actually felt and touched myself. It is a great trial, but I cannot help it, for I have no faith."

Just picture such a day as this, and see how disastrous it would be to yourself, and what utter folly it would appear to any one who should watch you through the whole of it. Realise how your friends would feel insulted, and how your servants would refuse to serve you another day. And then ask yourself the question, if this want of faith in your fellow-men would be so dreadful, and such utter folly, what must it be when you tell God that you have no power to trust Him nor to believe His word: that it is a great trial, but you cannot help it, for you have no faith

Is it possible that you can trust your fellow-men and cannot trust your God? That you can receive the "witness of men," and cannot receive the "witness of God?" That you can believe man's records; and cannot believe God's record? That you can commit your dearest earthly interests to your weak failing fellow creatures without a fear, and are afraid to commit your spiritual interests to the blessed Saviour who shed His blood for the very purpose of saving you, and who is declared to be "able to save you to the uttermost?"

Surely, surely, dear believer, you, whose very name of believer implies that you can believe, you will never again dare to excuse yourself on the plea of having no faith. For when you say this, you mean of course that you have no faith in God, for you are not asked to have faith in yourself, and you would be in a very wrong condition of soul if you had. Let me beg of you then, when you think or say these things, always to complete the sentence, and say, "I have no faith in God, I cannot believe God;" and this I am sure will soon become so dreadful to you, that you will not dare to continue it.

But, you say, I cannot believe without the Holy Spirit. Very well; will you conclude then that your want of faith is because of the failure of the blessed Spirit to do His work? For if it is, then surely you are not to blame, and need feel no condemnation, and all exhortations to you to believe are useless.

But, no! Do you not see that, in taking up this position,—that you have no faith and cannot believe,—you are not only "making God a liar," but you are also manifesting an utter want of confidence in the Holy Spirit. For He is always ready to help our infirmities. We never have to wait for Him, He is always waiting for us. And I for my part have such absolute confidence in the blessed Holy Ghost, and in His being always ready to do His work, that I dare to say to every one of you, that you *can* believe now, at this very moment, and that if you do not, it is not the Spirit's fault but your own.

Put your will then over on to the believing side.

Say, "Lord I will believe, I do believe," and continue to say it. Insist upon believing, in the face of every suggestion of doubt which. Satan may bring. Out of your very unbelief, throw yourself headlong on to the word and promises of God, and dare to abandon yourself to the keeping and saving power of the Lord Jesus. If you have ever trusted a precious interest in the bands of any earthly friend, I conjure you, trust yourself now and all your spiritual interest, in the hands of your Heavenly Friend, and never, *never,* NEVER, allow yourself to doubt again.

And remember, there are two things which are more utterly incompatible than even oil and water, and these two are trust and worry. Would you call it trust, if you should give something into the hands of a friend to attend to for you, and then should spend your nights and days in anxious thought and worry as to whether it would be rightly and successfully done? And can you call it trust, when you have given the saving and keeping of your soul into the hands of the Lord, if day lifter day and night after night you are spending hours of anxious thought and questionings about the matter? "When a believer really trusts anything, he ceases to worry about that thing which he has trusted. And when he worries it is a plain proof that he does not trust. Tested by this rule, how little real trust there is in the Church of Christ! No wonder our Lord asked the pathetic question, "When the Son of Man cometh shall He find faith on the earth?" He will find plenty of activity, a great deal of earnestness, and doubtless many consecrated hearts; but shall He find *faith*—the one thing He values more than all the rest? It is a solemn question, and I would that every Christian heart would ponder it well. But may the time past of our lives suffice us to have shared in the unbelief of the world, and may we every one, who know our blessed Lord and His unspeakable trustworthiness, set to our seal that He is true, by our generous abandonment of trust in Him.

I remember, very early in my Christian life, having every tender and loyal impulse within me stirred to its depths by an appeal I met with in a volume of old sermons, to all who loved the Lord Jesus, that they should show to others how worthy He was of being trusted, by the steadfastness of their own faith in Him. And I remember my soul cried out with an eager longing that I might be called to walk in paths so dark, that an utter abandonment of trust might be my blessed and glorious privilege.

"Ye have not passed this way heretofore," it may be; but to-day it is your happy privilege to prove, as never before, your loyal confidence in Jesus by starting out with Him on a life and walk of faith, lived moment by moment in absolute and childlike trust in Him.

You have trusted Him in a few things, and He has not failed you. Trust Him now for everything, and see if He does not do for you exceeding abundantly above all that you could ever have asked or thought, not according to your power or capacity, but according to His own mighty power, that will work in you all the good pleasure of His most blessed will.

You find no difficulty in trusting the Lord with the management of the universe and all the outward creation, and can your case be any more complex or difficult than these, that you need to be anxious or troubled about His management of it. Away with such unworthy doubtings! Take your stand on the power and trustworthiness of your God, and see how quickly all difficulties will vanish before a steadfast determination to believe. Trust in the dark, trust in the light, trust at night, and trust in the morning, and you will find that the faith, which may begin by a mighty effort, will end sooner or later by becoming the easy and natural habit of the soul.

All things are possible to God, and "all things are possible to him that believeth." Faith has, in times past, "subdued kingdoms, wrought righteousness, obtained promises, stopped the mouths of lions, quenched the violence of fire, escaped the edge of the sword, waxed valiant in fight, turned to flight the armies of the aliens;" and faith can do it again. For our Lord Himself says unto us, "If ye have faith as a grain of mustard seed, ye shall say unto this mountain, Remove hence to yonder place, and it shall remove; and nothing shall be impossible unto you."

If you are a child of God at all, you must have at least as much faith as a grain of mustard seed, and therefore you dare not say again that you cannot trust because you have no faith. Say rather, "I can trust my Lord, and I will trust Him, and not all the powers of earth or hell shall be able to make me doubt my wonderful, glorious, faithful Redeemer!"

Of all the worships we can bring Him, none is so sweet to Him as an utter self-abandoning trust. Let your faith then "throw its arms around all God has told you," and entreat Him to give you more to believe. And in every dark hour remember that "though now for a season, if need be, ye are in heaviness through manifold temptations," it is in order that "the trial of your faith, being much more precious than of gold that perisheth, though it be tried with fire, might be found unto praise, and honour, and glory, at the appearing; of Jesus Christ."

7

DIFFICULTIES CONCERN THE WILL

WHEN THE CHILD OF GOD has, by the way of entire abandonment and absolute trust, stepped out of himself into Christ, and has begun to know something of the blessedness of the life hid with Christ in God, there is one form of difficulty which is very likely to start up in his path. After the first emotions of peace and rest have somewhat subsided, or if, as is sometimes the case, they have never seemed to come at all, he begins to feel such an utter unreality in the things he has been passing through, that he seems to himself like a hypocrite when he says or even thinks they are real. It seems to him that his belief does not go below the surface—that it is a mere lip-belief, and therefore of no account, and that his surrender is not a surrender o1 the heart, and therefore cannot be acceptable to God. Ho is afraid to say he is altogether the Lord's, for fear he will be telling an untruth, and yet he cannot bring himself to say he is not, because he longs for it so intensely. The difficulty is real and very disheartening.

But there is nothing here which will not be very easily overcome, when the Christian once thoroughly understands the principles of the new life, and has learned *how* to live in it. The common thought *is*, that this life hid with Christ in God is to be lived in the emotions, and consequently all the attention of the soul is directed towards them, and as they are satisfactory or otherwise, the soul rests, or is troubled. Now the truth is that this life is not to be lived in the emotions at all, but in the will, and therefore the varying states of emotion do not in the least disturb or affect the reality of the life, if only the will is kept steadfastly abiding in its centre—God's will.

To make this plain, I must enlarge a little. Fenelon says, somewhere, that "pure religion resides in the will alone." By this he means that, as the will is the governing power in the man's nature, if the will is set straight, all the rest of the nature must come into harmony. By the will, I do not mean the wish of the man, nor even his purpose, but the choice, the deciding power, the king, to which all that is in the man must yield obedience. It is the man, in short—the *"Ego"*—that which we feel to be ourselves.

It is sometimes thought that the emotions are the governing power in our nature. But, as a matter of practical experience, I think we all of us know that there is something within us, behind our emotions, and behind our wishes—an independent self—that after all decides everything, and controls everything. Our emotions belong to us, and are suffered and enjoyed by us, but they are not ourselves; and if God is to take possession of us it must be into this central will or personality that He shall enter. If, then He is reigning there by the power of His Spirit, all the rest of our nature must come under His sway;—and as the will is, so is the man.

The practical bearing of this truth upon the difficulty I am considering is very great. For the decisions of our will are often so directly opposed to the decisions of our emotions that, if we are in the habit of considering our emotions as the test, we shall be very apt to feel like hypocrites in declaring those things to be real which our will alone has decided. But the moment we see that the will is king, we shall utterly disregard anything that clamours against.it, and shall claim as real its decisions, let the emotions rebel as they may.

I am aware that this is a difficult subject to deal with; but it is so exceedingly practical in its bearing upon the life of faith, that I beg of you, dear reader, not to turn from it until you have mastered it.

Perhaps an illustration will help you. A young man of great intelligence, seeking to enter into this new life, was utterly discouraged at finding himself the slave to an inveterate habit of doubting. To his emotions nothing seemed true, nothing seemed real; and the more he struggled the more unreal did it all become. He was told this secret concerning the will—that if he would only put his will over on to the believing side; if he would choose to believe; if, in short, he would, in the Ego of his nature, say, "I will believe! I do believe!" he need not trouble about his emotions, for they would find themselves compelled, sooner or later, to come into harmony, "What!" he said, "do you mean to tell me that I can *choose* to believe in that way, when nothing seems true to me; and will that kind of believing be real?" "Yes," was the answer, "your part is only this,—to put your will over on God's side in this matter of believing; and when you do this, God immediately takes possession of it, and works in you to will of His good pleasure, and you will soon find that He has brought all the rest of your nature into subjection to Himself." "Well," was the answer, "I can do this. I cannot control my emotions, but I can control my will, and the new life begins to look possible to me if it is only my will that needs to be set straight in the matter. I can give my will to God, and I do!" From that moment, disregarding all the pitiful clamouring of his emotions, that continually accused him of being a wretched hypocrite, this young man held on steadily to the decision of his will, answering every accusation with the continued assertion that he chose to believe, he meant to believe, he did believe; until at the end of a few days he found himself triumphant, with every emotion and every thought brought into captivity to the mighty power of the blessed Spirit of God, who had taken possession of the will thus put into His hands. He had held fast the *profession* of his faith without wavering, although it had seemed to him that, as to real faith itself, he had none to hold fast. At times it had drained all the will-power he possessed to his lips to Say that he believed, so contrary was it to all the evidence of his senses or of his emotions. But he had caught the idea that Ids will was, after all, himself, and that if he kept that on God's side, he was doing all he could do, and that God alone could change his emotions or control his being. The result has been one of the grandest Christian lives I know of, in its marvellous simplicity, directness, and power over sin.

The secret lies just here. That our will, which is the spring of all our actions, was in the fall handed over into the control of Satan, and he has been working it in us to our utter ruin and misery. Now God says, "Yield yourselves up unto Mo, as those that are alive from the dead, and

I will work in you to will and to do of my good pleasure." And the moment we yield ourselves, He of course takes possession of us, and does work in us "that -which is well pleasing in His sight through Jesus Christ," giving us the mind that was in Christ, and transforming us into His image (See Rom. 12:1, 2).

Let us take another illustration. A lady, who had entered into this life hid with Christ, was confronted by a great prospective trial. Every emotion she had "within her rose up in rebellion against it, and had she considered her emotions to be her king, she would have been in utter despair. But she had learned this secret of the will, and knowing that, at the bottom, she herself did really choose the will of God for her portion, she did not pay the slightest attention to her emotions, but persisted in meeting every thought concerning the trial with the words, repeated over and over, "Thy will be done! Thy will be done!" asserting, in the face of all her rebelling feelings, that she did submit her will to God's, that she chose to submit it, and that His will should be and was her delight! The result was, that in an incredibly short space of time every thought was brought into captivity, and she began to find even her very emotions rejoicing hi the will of God.

Again, there was a lady who had a besetting sin, which in her emotions she dearly loved, but which in her will she hated. Having believed herself to be necessarily under the control of her emotions, she had therefore thought she was unable to conquer it unless her emotions should first be changed. But she learned this secret concerning the will, and going to her knees she said, "Lord, Thou seest that with one part of my nature I love this sin, but in my real central self I hate it. And now I put my will over on Thy side in the matter. I will not do it any more. Do Thou deliver me." Immediately God took possession of the will thus surrendered to Himself, and began to work in her, so that His will in the matter gained the mastery over her emotions, and she found herself delivered, not by the power of an outward commandment, but by the inward power of the Spirit of God working in her that which was well pleasing in His sight.

And now, dear Christian, let me show you how to apply this principle to your difficulties. Cease to consider your emotions, for they are only the servants; and regard simply your will, which is the real king in your being. Is that given up to God? Is that put into His hands? Does your will decide to believe? Does your will chose to obey? If this is the case, then *you* are in the Lord's hands, and you decide to believe, and you choose to obey; for your will is yourself. And the thing is done. The transaction with God is as real, where only your will acts, as when every emotion coincides. It does not seem as real to you; but in God's sight it is as real. And when you have got hold of this secret, and have discovered that you need not attend to your emotions, but simply to the state of your will, all the Scripture commands—to yield yourself to God—to present yourself a living sacrifice to Him—to abide in Christ—to walk in the light—to die to self—become possible to you; for you are conscious that, in all these, your will can act, and can take God's side; whereas, if it had been your emotions that must do it, you would sink down in despair, knowing them to be utterly uncontrollable.

When, then, this feeling of unreality or hypocrisy comes, do not be troubled by it. It is only in your emotions, and is not worth a moment's thought. Only see to it that your will is in God's hands; that your inward self is abandoned to His working; that your choice, your decision, is on His side; and there leave it. Your surging emotions—like a tossing vessel, which, by degrees, yields to the steady pull of the cable— finding themselves attached to the mighty power of God by the choice of your will, must inevitably come into captivity, and give in their allegiance to Him, and you will verify the truth of the saying that, "If any man will do His will, he shall know of the doctrine."

The will is like a wise mother in a nursery; the feelings are like a set of clamouring crying children. The mother decides upon a certain course of action, which she believes to be right and best. The children clamour against it, and declare it shall not be. But the mother, knowing that she is mistress and not they, pursues her course calmly, unmoved by their clamours, and takes no notice of them except that of commanding them to be quiet. The result is that the children are sooner or later compelled to yield, and fall in with the decision of the mother. Thus order and harmony are preserved. But if that mother should for a moment let in the thought that the children were the mistresses instead of herself, confusion would reign unchecked. Such instances have been known in family life. And in how many souls at this very moment is there nothing but confusion, simply because the feelings are allowed to govern, instead of the will.

Remember, then, that the real thing in your experience is what your will decides, and not the verdict of your emotions; and that you are far more in danger of hypocrisy and untruth in yielding to the assertions of your feelings, than in holding fast to the decision of your will. So that, if your will is on God's side, you are no hypocrite at this moment in claiming as your own the blessed reality of belonging altogether to Him, even though your emotions may all declare the contrary.

I am convinced that, throughout the Bible, the expressions concerning the "heart" do not mean the emotions—that which we now understand by the word heart—but they mean the will, the personality of the man, the man's own central self; and that the object of God's dealings with man is that this "I" may be yielded up to Him, and this central life abandoned to His entire control. It is not the feelings of the man God wants, but the man himself.

Have you given Him yourself, dear reader? Have you abandoned your will to His working? Do you consent to surrender the very centre of your being into His hands? Then—let the outposts of your nature clamour as they may—it is your right to say, even now, with the Apostle, "I am crucified with Christ; nevertheless, I live; yet not I, but Christ liveth in me: and the life which I now live in the flesh, I live by the faith of the Son of God, who loved me, and gave Himself for me."

℘   ℭ

After this chapter had been enclosed to the printer, the following remarkable practical illustration of its teaching was presented by Pasteur

T. Monod, of Paris. It is the experience of a Presbyterian minister, which this Pasteur had carefully kept for many years.

Newburgh, September 26th, 1842.

DEAR BROTHER,——I take a few moments of that time which I have devoted to the Lord, in writing a short epistle to you His servant. It is sweet to feel we are wholly the Lord's, that He has received us and called us His. This is religion——a relinquishment of the principle of self-ownership, and the adoption in full of the abiding sentiment: "I am not my own, I am bought with a price." Since I last saw you, I have been pressing forward, and yet there has been nothing remarkable in my experience of which I can speak; indeed I do not know that it is best to look for remarkable things; but *strive to be* holy, as God is holy, pressing right on toward the mark of the prize.

I do not feel myself qualified to instruct you: I can only tell you the way in which I was led. The Lord deals differently with different souls, and we ought not to attempt to copy the experience of others, yet there are certain things which must be attended to by every one who is seeking after a clean heart.

There must be a personal consecration, of all to God, a covenant made with God, that we will be wholly and for ever His. This I made intellectually without any change in my feelings——with a heart full of hardness and darkness, unbelief and sin, and insensibility.

I covenanted to be the Lord's, and laid all upon the altar, a living sacrifice, to the best of my ability. And after I rose from my knees, I was conscious of no change in my feelings. I was painfully conscious that there was no change. But yet I was sure that I did, with all the sincerity and honesty of purpose of which I was capable, make an entire and eternal consecration of myself to God. I did not then consider the work as done by any means——but I engaged to abide in a state of entire devotion to God——a living perpetual sacrifice. And now came the effort to do this.

I knew that I must believe that God did accept me, and did come in to dwell in my heart. I was conscious I did not believe this, and yet I desired to do so. I read with much prayer John's first Epistle, and endeavoured to assure my heart of God's love to me as an individual. I was sensible that my heart was full of evil. I seemed to have no power to overcome pride, or to repel evil thoughts which I abhorred. But Christ was manifested to destroy the works of the devil, and it was clear that the sin in my heart was the work of the devil. I was enabled, therefore, to believe that God was working in me, to will and to do, while I was working out my own salvation with fear and trembling.

I was convinced of unbelief, that it was *voluntary and criminal.* I clearly saw that unbelief was an awful sin—it made the faithful God a liar. The Lord brought before me my besetting sins which had dominion over me, especially preaching myself instead of Christ, and indulging self-complacent thoughts after preaching. I was enabled to make myself of no reputation, and to seek the honour which cometh from God only. Satan struggled hard to beat me back from the Rock of Ages, but thanks to God I finally hit upon the method of living by the moment, and then I found rest.

I trusted in the blood of Jesus already shed, as a sufficient atonement for all my past sins, and the future I committed wholly to the Lord, agreeing to do His will under all circumstances as He should make it known, and I saw that all I had to do was to look to Jesus for a present supply of grace, and to trust Him to cleanse my heart and keep me from sin at the present moment.

I felt shut up to a momentary dependence upon the grace of Christ. I would not permit the adversary to trouble me about the past or future, for I each moment looked for the supply for that moment. I agreed that I would be a child of Abraham and walk by naked faith in the Word of God, and not by inward feelings and emotions—I would seek to be a Bible Christian. Since that time the Lord has given me a steady victory over sins which before enslaved me. I delight in the Lord, and in His Word. I delight in my work as a minister—my fellowship is with the Father and with His Son Jesus Christ. I am a babe in Christ; I know my progress has been small compared with that made by many. My feelings vary, but when I have feelings, I praise God, and I trust in His word, and when I am empty and my feelings are gone, I do the same. I have covenanted to walk by faith and not by feelings.

The Lord, I think, is beginning to revive His work among my people. "Praise the Lord." May the Lord fill you with all His fulness and give you all the mind of Christ. O be faithful! Walk before God and be perfect. Preach the Word. Be instant in season and out of season. The Lord loves you. He works with you. Rest your soul fully upon that promise, "Lo I am with you alway, even unto the end of the world."

Your fellow-soldier,
WILLIAM HILL.

There may be some who will object to this teaching that it ignores the work of the blessed Holy Spirit. But I must refer such to the introductory chapter of this book, in which I have fully explained myself. I am not writing upon that side of the subject; I am considering man's part in the matter, and not the part of the Spirit. I realize intensely that all a man can do or try to do would be utterly useless, if the Holy Spirit did not work in that man continually. And it is only because I believe in the Spirit as a mighty power, ever present and always ready to do his work, that I can write as I do. But, like the wind that bloweth where it listeth, and thou hearest the sound thereof, but canst not tell whence it cometh, and whether it goeth, the operations of the Spirit are beyond our control, and also beyond our comprehension. The results we know, and the steps on our part which lead to those results, but we know nothing more. And yet, like a workman in a great manufactory, who does not question the commands of his employer, and is not afraid to undertake apparent impossibilities, because he knows there is a mighty unseen power, called steam, behind his machinery, which can accomplish it all, so we dare to urge upon men that they shall simply and courageously set themselves to do that which they are commanded to do, because we know that the mighty Spirit will never fail to supply at each moment the necessary power for that moment's act. And we boldly claim that we who thus write, can say from our very hearts, as earnestly and as solemnly as any other Christians, We believe in the Holy Ghost.

8

IS GOD IN EVERYTHING?

ONE OF THE GREATEST obstacles to living unwaveringly this life of entire surrender, is the difficulty of seeing God in everything. People say, "I can easily submit to things which come from God; but I cannot submit to man, and most of my trials and crosses come through human instrumentality." Or they say, "It is all well enough to talk of trusting; but when I commit a matter to God, man is sure to come in and disarrange it all; and while I have no difficulty in trusting God, I do see serious difficulties in the way of trusting men."

This is no imaginary trouble, but it is of vital importance, and if it cannot be met, does really make the life of faith an impossible and visionary theory. For nearly everything in life comes to us through human instrumentalities, and most of our trials are the result of somebody's failure, or ignorance, or carelessness, or sin. We know God cannot be the author of these things, and yet unless He is the agent in the matter, how can we say to Him about it, "Thy will be done?"

Besides, what good is there in trusting our affairs to God, if, after all, man is to be allowed to come in and disarrange them; and how is it possible to live by faith, if human agencies, in whom it would be wrong and foolish to trust, are to have a predominant influence in moulding our lives?

Moreover, things in which we can see God's hand always have a sweetness in them which consoles while it wounds. But the trials inflicted by man are full of bitterness.

What is needed, then, is to see *God in everything*, and to receive everything directly from His hands, with no intervention of second causes. And it is just to this that we must be brought, before we can know an abiding experience of entire abandonment and perfect trust. Our abandonment must be *to God*, not to man, and our trust must be in Him, not in any arm of flesh, or we shall fail at the first trial.

The question here confronts us at once—"But *is* God in everything, and have we any warrant from the Scripture for receiving everything from His hands, without regarding the second causes which may have been instrumental in bringing it about?" I answer to this, unhesitatingly, YES. To the children of God everything comes directly from their Father's hand, no matter who or what may have been the apparent agents. There are no "second causes" for them.

The whole teaching of the Scripture asserts and implies this. "Not a sparrow falls to the ground without our Father. The very hairs of our head are all numbered." We are not to be careful about any thing, because our Father cares for us. We are not to avenge ourselves, because our Father has charged Himself *with* our defence. We are not to fear, for the Lord is on our side. No one can be against us, because He is for us. We shall not want, for He is our Shepherd. When we pass through the rivers they shall not overflow us, and when we walk through the fire we shall not be burned, because He will be with us. He shuts the mouths of lions, that they cannot hurt us. "He delivereth and rescueth." "He changeth the times and the seasons; He removeth kings and setteth up kings." A man's heart is in His hand, and, "as the rivers of water, He turneth it withersoever He will." He ruleth over all the kingdoms of the heathen; and in His hand there is power and might, "so that none is able to withstand" Him. "He ruleth the raging of the sea; when the waves thereof arise He stilleth them." He "bringeth the counsel of the heathen to nought; He maketh the devices of the people of none effect." "Whatsoever the Lord pleaseth, that does He in heaven, and in earth, in the seas, and all deep places."

"If thou seest the oppression of the poor, and violent perverting of judgment and justice in a province, marvel not at the matter; for He that is higher than the highest regardeth; and there be higher than they."

"Lo, these are a part of His ways; but how little a portion is heard of Him? But the thunder of His power who can understand?" "Hast thou not known, hast thou not heard, that the everlasting God, the Lord, the Creator of the ends of the earth, fainteth not, neither is weary? There is no searching of His understanding."

ιis "God is our refuge and strength, a very present help in
ιerefore mil not we fear, though the earth be removed, and
ιe mountains be carried into the midst of the sea; though the
wateɪ₃ ιereof roar and be troubled; though the mountains shake with
the swelling thereof" "I will say of the Lord He is my refuge and my
fortress, my God, in Him will I trust. Surely He shall deliver thee from
the snare of the fowler, and from the noisome pestilence. He shall cover
thee with His feathers, and under His wings shalt thou trust. His truth
shall be thy shield and buckler. Thou shalt not be afraid for the terror by
night, nor for the arrow that flieth by day, nor for the pestilence that
walketh in darkness, nor for the destruction that wasteth at noonday. A
thousand shall fall at thy side, and ten thousand at thy right hand; but it
shall not come nigh thee." "Because thou hast made the Lord, which is
my refuge, even the Most High thy habitation, there shall no evil befall
thee, neither shall any plague come nigh thy dwelling. For He shall give
His angels charge over thee, to keep thee in all thy ways."

To my own mind, these Scriptures, and many others like them,
settle for ever the question as to the power of second causes in the life
of the children of God. They are all under the control of our Father, and
nothing can touch us except with His knowledge, and by His
permission. It may be the sin of man that originates the action, and
therefore the thing itself cannot be said to be the will of God; but by the
time it reaches us, it has become God's will for us, and must *he* accepted
as directly from His hands. No man or company of men, no power in
earth or heaven, can touch that soul which is abiding in Christ, without
first passing through Him, and receiving the seal of His permission. If
God be for us, it matters not who may be against us; nothing can disturb
or harm us, except He shall see that it is best for us, and shall stand aside
to let it pass.

An earthly parent's care for his helpless child is a feeble illustration
of this. If the child is in its father's arms, nothing can touch it without
that father's consent, unless he is too weak to prevent it. And even if
this should be the case, he suffers the harm first in his own person,
before he allows it to reach his child. And if an earthly parent would

thus care for his little helpless one, how much more will our Heavenly Father, whose love is infinitely greater, and whose strength and wisdom can never be baffled? I am afraid there are some, even of God's own children, who scarcely think that He is equal to themselves in tenderness, and love, and thoughtful care; and who, in their secret thoughts, charge Him with a neglect and indifference of which they would feel themselves incapable. The truth really is, that His care is infinitely superior to any possibilities of human care: and that He who counts the very hairs of our heads, and suffers not a sparrow to fall without Him, takes note of the minutest matters that can affect the lives of His children, and regulates them all according to His own sweet will, let their origin be what they may.

The instances of this are numberless. Take Joseph. What could have seemed more apparently on the face of it to be the result of sin, and utterly contrary to the will of God, than his being sold into slavery? And yet Joseph in speaking of it said, "As for you, ye thought evil against me; but God meant it unto good." "Now, therefore, be not grieved nor angry with yourselves, that ye sold me hither, for God did send me before you to preserve life." To the eye of sense it was surely Joseph's wicked brethren who had sent him into Egypt, and yet Joseph, looking at it with the eye of faith, could say, "God sent me." It had been undoubtedly a grievous sin in his brethren, but, by the time it had reached Joseph, it had become God's will for him, and was in truth, though at first it did not look so, the greatest blessing of his whole life. And thus we see how the Lord can make even the wrath of man to praise Him, and how all things, even the sins of others, shall work together for good to them that love Him.

I learned this lesson practically and experimentally long years before I knew the Scriptural truth concerning it. I was attending a prayer-meeting held for the promotion of Scriptural holiness, when a strange lady rose to speak, and I looked at her wondering who she could be, little thinking she was to bring a message to my soul which would teach me such a grand lesson. She said she had great difficulty in living the life of faith, on account of the second causes that seemed to her to control nearly everything that concerned her. Her perplexity became so great that at last she began to ask God to teach her the truth about it, whether He really was in everything or not. After praying this for a few days, she had what she described as a vision. She thought she was in a perfectly dark place, and that there advanced towards her from a distance a body of light, which gradually surrounded and enveloped her and everything around her. As it approached, a voice seemed to say, "This is the presence of God—this is the presence of God." While surrounded with this presence, all the great and awful things in life seemed to pass before her—fighting armies, wicked men, raging beasts, storms and pestilences, sin and suffering of every kind. She shrank back at first in terror, but she soon saw that the Presence of God so surrounded and enveloped each one of these, that not a lion could reach out its paw, nor a bullet fly through the air, except as His Presence moved out of the way to permit it. And she saw, that let there be ever so thin a sheet, as it were, of this glorious Presence between herself and the most terrible violence, not a hair of her head could be ruffled, nor anything touch her, unless the Presence divided to let the evil through. Then all the small and annoying things of life passed before her, and equally she saw that these also were so enveloped in this Presence of God, that not a cross look, nor a harsh word, nor petty trial of any kind, could reach her unless His Presence moved out of the way to let it.

Her difficulty vanished. Her question was answered for ever. God was in everything; and to her henceforth there were no second causes. She saw that her life came to her day by day and hour by hour directly from His hand, let the agencies which should seem to control it be what they might. And never again had she found any difficulty in an abiding consent to His will, and an unwavering trust in His care.

If we look at the seen things, we shall not be able to understand the secret of this. But the children of God are called to look "not at the things which are seen: for the things which are seen are temporal; but the things which are not seen are eternal." Could we but see with our bodily eyes His unseen forces surrounding us on every side, we would walk through this world in an impregnable fortress, which nothing could ever overthrow or penetrate, for "the angel of the Lord encampeth round about them that fear Him, and delivereth them."

We have a striking illustration of this in the history of Elisha. The King of Syria was warring against Israel, but his evil designs were continually frustrated by the prophet, and at last he sent his army to the prophet's own city for the express purpose of taking him captive. We read, "He sent thither horses, and chariots, and a great host: and they came by night, and compassed the city about." This was the seen thing. And the servant of the prophet, whose eyes had not yet been opened to see the unseen things, was alarmed. And we read, "And when the servant of the man of God was risen early, and gone forth, behold an host compassed the city, both with horses and chariots. And his servant said unto him, Alas, my master! how shall we do?" But his master could see the unseen things, and he replied, "Fear not; for they that be with us are more than they that be with them." And then he prayed, saying, "Lord, I pray thee, open his eyes that he may see. And the Lord opened the eyes of the young man; and he saw: and, behold, the mountain was full of horses and chariots of fire round about Elisha."

The presence of God is the fortress of His people. Nothing can withstand it. At His presence the wicked perish; the earth trembles; the hills melt like wax; the cities are broken down; "the heavens also dropped, and Sinai itself was moved at the presence of God." And in the secret of this presence He has promised to hide His people from the pride of man, and from the strife of tongues. "My presence shall go with thee," He says, "and I will give thee rest."

I wish it were only possible to make every Christian see this truth as plainly as I see it. For I am convinced it is the only clue to a completely restful life. Nothing else will enable a soul to live only in the present moment as we are commanded to do, and to take no thought for the morrow. Nothing else will take all the risks and "supposes" out of a Christian's life, and enable him to say, "Surely goodness and mercy shall follow me all the days of my life." Abiding in God's presence we run no risks. And such a soul can triumphantly say—

"I know not what it is to doubt,
My heart is always gay;
I run no risks, for, come what will,
God always has His way!"

I once heard of a poor coloured woman, who earned a precarious living by daily labour, but who was a joyous triumphant Christian. "Ah, Nancy," said a gloomy Christian lady to her one day, who almost disapproved of her constant cheerfulness, and yet envied it,—"Ah, Nancy, it is all well enough to be happy now; but I should think the thoughts of your future would sober you. Only suppose, for instance, that you should have a spell of sickness, and be unable to work; or suppose your present employers should move away, and no one else should give you anything to do; or suppose—" "Stop!" cried Nancy, "I never supposes. De Lord is my Shepherd, and I knows I shall not want. And, honey," she added to her gloomy friend, "it's all dem *supposes* as is makin' you so mis'able. You'd better give dem all up, and just trust de Lord."

There is one text that will take all the "supposes" out of a believer's life, if only it is received and acted on in childlike faith: it is Heb. 13:5,6—"Be content, therefore, with such things as ye have; for He hath said, I will never leave thee, nor forsake thee. So that we may boldly say,

"The Lord is my Helper, and I fear not what man shall do unto me."

What if dangers of all sorts shall threaten you from every side, and the malice, or foolishness, or ignorance of men shall combine to do you harm? You may face every possible contingency with these triumphant words, "The Lord is my helper, and I will not fear what man shall do unto me." If the Lord is your helper, how *can* you fear what man may do unto you? There is no man in this world, nor company of men, that can touch you, unless your God in whom you trust shall please to let them. "He will not suffer thy foot to be moved: He that keepeth thee will not slumber. Behold He that keepeth Israel shall neither slumber nor sleep.

66

The Lord is thy keeper; the Lord is thy shade upon thy right hand. The sun shall not smite thee by day, nor the moon by night. The Lord shall preserve thee from all evil: He shall preserve thy soul. The Lord shall preserve thy going out, and thy coming in, from this time forth, and even for evermore."

Nothing else but this seeing God in everything will make us loving and patient with those who annoy and trouble us. They will be to us then only the instruments for accomplishing His tender and wise purposes towards us, and we shall even find ourselves at last inwardly thanking them for the blessings they bring us.

Nothing else will completely put an end to all murmuring or rebelling thoughts. Christians often feel a liberty to murmur against man when they would not dare to murmur against God. But this way of receiving things would make it impossible ever to murmur. If our Father permits a trial to come, it must be because that trial is the sweetest and best thing that could happen to us, and we must accept it with thanks from His dear hand. The trial itself may be hard to flesh and blood, and I do not mean that we can like or enjoy the suffering of it. But we can and must love the will of God *in* the trial, for His will is always sweet whether it be in joy or in sorrow.

In short, this way of seeing our Father in everything makes life one long thanksgiving, and gives a rest of heart, and, more than that, a gaiety of spirit that is unspeakable. Some one says, "God's will on earth is always joy, always tranquility." And since He must have His own way concerning His children, into what wonderful green pastures of inward rest, and beside what blessedly still waters of inward refreshment is the soul led that learns this secret.

If the will of God is our will, and if He always has His way, then we always have our way also, and we reign in a perpetual kingdom. He who sides with God cannot fail to win in every encounter; and whether the result shall be joy or sorrow, failure or success, death or life, we may, under all circumstances, join in the Apostle's shout of victory, "Thanks be unto God which always causeth us to triumph in Christ!"

9

GROWTH

WHEN THE BELIEVER HAS BEEN brought to the point of entire surrender and perfect trust, and finds himself dwelling and walking in a life of happy communion and perfect peace, the question naturally arises, "Is this the end?" I answer emphatically, "No, it is only the beginning."

And yet this is so little understood, that one of the greatest objections made against the advocates of this life of faith, is, that they do not believe in growth in grace. They are supposed to teach that the soul arrives at a state of perfection beyond which there is no advance, and that all the exhortations in the Scripture which point towards growth and development are rendered void by this teaching.

As exactly the opposite of this is true, I have thought it important next to consider this subject carefully, that I may, if possible, fully answer such objections, and may also show what is the Scriptural place to grow in, and how the soul is to grow. The text which is most frequently quoted is 2 Pet. 3:18, "But grow in grace, and in the knowledge of our Lord and Saviour Jesus Christ." Now, this text exactly expresses what we believe to be God's will for us, and what also we believe He has made it possible for us to experience. We accept, in their very fullest meaning, all the commands and promises concerning our being no more children, and our growing up into Christ in all things, until we come unto a perfect man, unto the measure of the stature of the fulness of Christ. We rejoice that we need not continue always to be babes, needing milk, but that we may, by reason of use and development, become such as have need of strong meat, skilful in the word of righteousness, and able to discern both good and evil. And none would grieve more than we at the thought of any finality in the Christian life, beyond which there could be no advance.

But then we believe in a growing that does really produce maturity, and in a development that, as a fact, does bring forth ripe fruit. We expect to reach the aim set before us, and if we do not, we feel sure there must be some fault in our growing. No parent would be satisfied with the growth of his child, if, day after day, and year after year, it remained the same helpless babe it was in the first months of its life. And no farmer would feel comfortable under such growing of his grain, as should stop short at the blade, and never produce the ear, nor the full corn in the ear. Growth, to be real, must be progressive, and the days, and weeks, and months must see a development and increase of maturity in the thing growing. But is this the case with a large part of that which is called growth in grace? Does not the very Christian who is the most strenuous in his longings and in his efforts after it, too often find that at the end of the year he is not as far on in his Christian experience as at the beginning, and that his zeal, and his devotedness, and his separation from the world, are not as whole-souled, or complete, as when his Christian life first began?

I was once urging upon a company of Christians the privileges and rest of an immediate and definite step into the land of promise, when a lady of great intelligence interrupted me with what she evidently felt to be a complete rebuttal of all I had been saying; exclaiming, "Ah! but my dear friend, I believe in *growing* in grace." "How long have you been growing?" I asked. "About twenty-five years," was her answer. "And how much more unworldly and devoted to the Lord are you now than when you began your Christian life?" I continued. "Alas!" was the answer, "I fear I am not nearly so much so;" and with this answer her eyes were opened to see that at all events her way of growing had not been successful, but quite the reverse.

The trouble with her, and every other such case, is simply this— they are trying to grow *into* grace, instead of *in* it. They are like a rosebush which the gardener should plant in the hard, stony path with a view to its growing *into* the flower-bed, and which would of course dwindle and wither in consequence, instead of flourishing and maturing. The Children of Israel wandering in the wilderness are a perfect picture of this sort of growing. They were travelling about for forty years, taking many weary steps, and finding but little rest from their wanderings, and yet, at the end of it all, were no nearer the promised land than they were at the beginning. When they started on their wanderings at Kadesh Barnea they were at the borders of the land, and a few steps would have taken them into it. When they ended their wanderings in the plains of Moab they were also at its borders; only with this great difference, that now there was a river to cross which at first there would not have been. All their wanderings and fightings in the wilderness had not put them in possession of one inch of the promised land. In order to get possession of this land it was necessary first to be in it. And in order to grow in grace, it is necessary first to be planted in grace. But when once in the land, their conquest was very rapid; and when once planted in grace, the growth of the soul in one month will exceed that of years in any other soil. For grace is a most fruitful soil, and the plants that grow therein are plants of a marvellous growth. They are tended by a Divine Husbandman, and are warmed by the Sun of Righteousness, and watered by the dew from Heaven. Surely it is no wonder that they bring forth fruit, "some an hundred-fold, some sixty-fold, some thirty-fold."

But, it will be asked, What is meant by growing in grace? It is difficult to answer this question, because so few people have any conception of what the grace of God really is. To say that it is free, unmerited favour, only expresses a little of its meaning. It is the wondrous, boundless love of God, poured out upon us without stint or measure, not according to our deserving, hut according to His infinite heart of love, which passeth knowledge, so unfathomable are its heights and depths. I sometimes think we give a totally different meaning to the word love when it is associated with God, from that we so well understand in its human application. But if ever human love was tender, and self-sacrificing and devoted; if ever it could bear and forbear; if ever it could suffer gladly for its loved ones; if ever it was willing to pour itself out in a lavish abandonment for the comfort or pleasure of its objects; then infinitely more is Divine love tender, and self-sacrificing and devoted, and glad to bear and forbear, and to suffer, and to lavish its best of gifts and blessings upon the objects of its love. Put together all the tenderest love you know of, dear reader, the deepest you have ever felt, and the strongest that has ever been poured out upon you, and heap upon it all the love of all the loving human hearts in the world, and then multiply it by infinity, and you will begin perhaps to have some faint glimpses of what the love of God in Christ Jesus is. And this is grace. And to be planted in grace is to live in the very heart of this love, to be enveloped by it, to be steeped in it, to revel in it, to know nothing else but love only and love always, to grow day by day in the knowledge of it, and in faith in it, to entrust everything to its care, and to have no shadow of a doubt but that it will surely order all things well.

To grow in grace is opposed to all self-dependence, to all self effort, to all legality of every kind. It is to put our growing, as well as everything else, into the hands of the Lord, and leave it with Him. It is to be satisfied with our Husbandman, and with His skill and wisdom, that not a question will cross our minds as to His modes of treatment, or His plan of cultivation. It is to grow as the lilies grow, or as the babes grow, without a care and without anxiety; to grow by the power of an inward-life principle that cannot help but grow; to grow because we live and therefore must grow; to grow because He who has planted us has planted a growing thing, and has made us to grow.

Surely this is what our Lord meant when He said, "Consider the lilies, how they grow; they toil not, neither do they spin: and yet I say unto you, that even Solomon in all his glory was not arrayed like one of these." Or, when He says again, "Which of you by taking thought can add one cubit unto his stature?" There is no effort in the growing of a child or of a lily. They do not toil nor spin, they do not stretch nor strain, they do not make any effort of any kind to grow; they are not conscious even that they are growing; but by an inward-life principle, and through the nurturing care of God's providence, and the fostering of care-taker or gardener, by the heat of the sun and the falling of the rain, they grow and grow.

And the result is sure. Even Solomon, our Lord says, in all his glory was not arrayed like one of these. Solomon's array cost much toiling and spinning, and gold and silver in abundance; but the lily's array cost none of these. And though we may toil and spin to make for ourselves beautiful spiritual garments, and may strain and stretch in our efforts after spiritual growth, we shall accomplish nothing; for no man by taking thought *can* add one cubit to his stature, and no array of ours can ever equal the beautiful dress with which the great Husbandman clothes the plants that grow in His garden of grace, and under His fostering care.

If I could but make each one of my readers realize how utterly helpless we are in this matter of growing, I am convinced a large part of the strain would be taken out of many lives at once. Imagine a child possessed of the monomania that he would not grow unless he made some personal effort after it, and who should insist upon a combination of ropes and pulleys whereby to stretch himself up to the desired height. He might, it is true, spend his days and years in a weary strain, but after all there would be no change in the inexorable fiat, "No man by taking thought can add one cubit unto his stature;" and his years of labour would be only wasted, if they did not really hinder the longed-for end.

Imagine a lily trying to clothe itself in beautiful colours and graceful lines, stretching its leaves and stems to make them grow, and seeking to manage the clouds and the sunshine, that its needs might be all judiciously supplied!

And yet in these two pictures we have, I conceive, only too true a picture of what many Christians are trying to do, who knowing they ought to grow, and feeling within them an instinct that longs for growth, yet think to accomplish it by toiling, and spinning, and stretching, and straining, and pass their lives in such a round of self-effort as is a weariness to contemplate.

Grow, dear friends; but grow I beseech you in God's way, which is the only effectual way. See to it that you are planted in grace, and then let the Divine Husbandman cultivate you in His own way and by His own means. Put yourselves out in the sunshine of His presence, and let the dew of Heaven come down upon you, and see what will come of it. Leaves, and flowers, and fruit must surely come in their season; for your Husbandman is a skilful one, and He never fails in His harvesting. Only see to it that you oppose no hindrance to the shining of the Sun of Righteousness, or the falling of the dew from Heaven. A very thin covering may serve to keep off the heat or the moisture, and the plant may wither even in their midst. And the slightest barrier between your soul and Christ may cause you to dwindle and fade, as a plant in a cellar, or under a bushel. Keep the sky clear. Open wide every avenue of your being to receive the blessed influences your Divine Husbandman may bring to bear upon you. Bask in the sunshine of His love. Drink in of the waters of His goodness. Keep your face upturned to Him. Look, and your soul shall live.

You need make no efforts to grow. But let your efforts instead be all concentrated on this, that you abide in the vine. The Husbandman who has the care of the vine will care for its branches also, and will so prune, and purge, and water, and tend them, that they will grow and bring forth fruit, and their fruit shall remain; and, like the lily, they shall find themselves arrayed in apparel so glorious, that that of Solomon will be as nothing to it.

What if you seem to yourselves to be planted at this moment in a desert soil, where nothing can grow. Put yourselves absolutely into the hands of the great Husbandman, and He will at once make that desert blossom as the rose, and will cause springs and fountains of water to start up out of its sandy wastes. For the promise is sure, that the man who trusts in the Lord "shall be as a tree planted by the waters, and that spreadeth out her roots by the river, and shall not see when heat cometh, but her leaf shall be green; and shall not be careful in the year of drought, neither shall cease from yielding fruit." It is the great prerogative of our Divine Husbandman that He is able to turn any soil, whatever it may be like, into the soil of grace, the moment we put our growing into His hands. He does not need to transplant us into a different field, but right where we are, with just the circumstances that surround us, He makes His sun to shine and His dew to fall upon us, and transforms the very things that were before our greatest hindrances, into the chiefest and most Messed means of our growth. I care not what the circumstances may be, His wonder-working power can accomplish this. And we must trust Trim with it all. Surely He is a Husbandman we *can* trust. And if He sends storms, or winds, or rains, or sunshine, all must be accepted at His hands, with the most unwavering confidence that He who has undertaken to cultivate. us, and to bring us to maturity, knows the very best way of accomplishing His end, and regulates the elements, which are all at His disposal, expressly with a view to our most rapid growth.

Let me entreat of you, then, to give up all your efforts after growing, and simply to *let* yourselves grow. Leave it all to the Husbandman, whose care it is, and who alone is able to manage it. No difficulties in your case can baffle Him. No dwarfing of your growth in years that are past, no apparent dryness of your inward springs of life, no crookedness or deformity in any of your past development, can in the least mar the perfect work that He will accomplish, if you will only put yourselves absolutely into His hands, and let Him have His own way with you. His own gracious promise to His backsliding children assures you of this. "I will heal their backsliding," He says: "I will love them freely, for mine anger is turned away from him. I will be as the dew unto Israel; he shall grow as the lily, and cast forth his roots as Lebanon. His branches shall spread, and his beauty shall be as the olive-tree, and his smell as Lebanon. They that dwell under his shadow shall return; they shall revive as the corn, and grow as the vine: the scent thereof shall be as the wine of Lebanon." And again, he says: "Be not afraid, for the pastures of the wilderness do spring, for the tree bareth her fruit, the fig tree and the vine do yield their strength. And the floors shall be full of wheat, and the fats shall overflow with wine and oil. And I will restore to you the years that the locust hath eaten. And ye shall eat in plenty, and be satisfied, and praise the name of the Lord your God, who hath dealt wondrously with you; and my people shall never be ashamed."

Oh, that you could but know just what your Lord meant when He said, "Consider the lilies, *how they grow;* for they toil not, neither do they spin." Surely these words give us a picture of a life and of a growth far different from the ordinary life and growth of Christians—a life of rest, and a growth without effort, and yet a life and a growth crowned with glorious results. And to every soul that will thus become a lily in the garden of the Lord, and will grow as the lilies grow, the same glorious array will be surely given as is given them; and they will know the fulfilment if that wonderful mystical passage concerning their Beloved, that "He feedeth among the lilies."

This is the sort of growth in grace in which we who have entered into the life of full trust believe; a growth which brings the desired results, which blossoms out into flower and fruit, and becomes lite a tree planted by the rivers of water, that bringeth forth his fruit in his season; whose leaf also does not wither, and who prospers in whatsoever he doeth. And we rejoice to know that there are growing up now in the Lord's heritage many such plants, who, as the lilies behold the face of the sun and grow thereby, are, by beholding as in a glass the glory of the Lord, being changed into the same image from glory to glory, even as by the spirit of the Lord.

Should you ask such, how it is that they grow so rapidly, and with such success; their answer would be that they are not concerned about their growing, and are hardly conscious that they do grow. That their Lord has told them to abide in Him, and has promised that, if they do thus abide, they shall certainly bring forth much fruit; and that they are concerned only about the abiding, which is their part, and leave the cultivating, and the growing, and the training, and pruning, to their good Husbandman, who alone is able to manage these things, or bring them about. You will find that such souls are not engaged in watching self, but in looking unto Jesus. They do not toil, nor spin for their spiritual garments, but leave themselves in the hands of the Lord, to be arrayed as it may please Him. Self-effort, and self-dependence, are at an end with them. Their interest in self is gone, transferred over into the hands of another. Self has become really nothing, and Christ alone is all in all to such as these. And the blessed result is that not even Solomon, in all his glory, was arrayed like these shall be.

I will close with a few practical words. We all know that growing is not a thing of effort, but is the result of an inward life—a principle of growth. All the stretching and pulling in the world could not make a dead oak grow. But a live oak grows without stretching. It is plain, therefore, that the essential thing is to get within you the growing life, and then you cannot help but grow. And this life is the life hid with Christ in God, the wonderful divine life of an indwelling Holy Ghost. Be filled with this, dear believer, and, whether you are conscious of it or not, you must grow—you cannot help growing. Do not trouble about your growing, but see to it that you have the growing life. Abide in the Vine. Let the life from Him flow through all your spiritual veins. Interpose no barrier to His mighty life-giving power, working in you all the good pleasure of His will. Yield yourself up utterly to His sweet control. Put your growing into His hands as completely as you have put all your other affairs. Suffer Him to manage it as He will. Do not concern yourself about it, nor even think of it. Trust Him absolutely, and always. Accept each moment's dispensation as it comes to you, from His dear hands, as being the needed sunshine or dew for that moment's growth. Say a continual "Yes" to your Father's will. And finally in this, as in all the other cares of your life, "Be careful for nothing; but in everything, by prayer and supplication, with thanksgiving, let your requests be made known unto God. And the peace of God that passeth all understanding shall keep your hearts and minds through Christ Jesus."

And the blessed result of this will be, that you shall know a literal fulfilment of the promise, "The righteous shall flourish like the palmtree: he shall grow like a cedar in Lebanon. Those that be planted in the house of the Lord shall flourish in the courts of our God. They shall bring forth fruit in old age; they shall be fat and flourishing."

10

SERVICE

THERE IS, PERHAPS, NO PART of Christian experience where a greater change is known upon entering into the life hid with Christ in God, than in the matter of service.

In all the lower forms of Christian life, service is apt to have more or less of bondage in it—that is, it is done purely as a matter of duty, and often as a trial and a cross. Certain things, which at the first may have been a joy and a delight, become weary tasks—performed faithfully perhaps, but with much secret disinclination, and many confessed or unconfessed wishes that they need not be done at all, or at least that they need not be done so often. The soul finds itself saying, instead of the "May I" of love, the "Must I" of duty. The yoke, which was at first easy, begins to gall, and the burden feels heavy instead of light.

One dear Christian expressed it once to me in this way. "When I was first converted," she said, "I was so full of joy and love that I was only too glad and thankful to be allowed to do anything for my Lord, and I eagerly entered every open door. But after awhile, as my early joy faded away, and my love burned less fervently, I began to wish I had not been quite so eager; for I found myself involved in lines of service which were gradually becoming very distasteful and burdensome to me. I could not very well give them up, since I had begun them, without exciting great remark, and yet I longed to do so increasingly. I was expected to visit the sick, and pray beside their beds. I was expected to attend prayer meetings, and speak at them. I was expected to be always ready for every effort in Christian work, and the sense of these expectations bowed me down continually. At last it became so unspeakably burdensome to me to live the sort of Christian life I had entered upon, and was expected by all around me to live, that I felt as if any kind of manual labour would have been easier, and I would have preferred, infinitely, scrubbing all day on my hands and knees to being compelled to go through the treadmill of my daily Christian work. I envied," she said, "the servants in the kitchen, and the women at the wash-tubs."

This may seem to some like a strong statement: but does it not present a vivid picture of some of your own experiences, dear Christian? Have you never gone to your work as a slave to his daily task, knowing it to be your duty, and that therefore you must do it, but rebounding like an india-rubber ball back into your real interests and pleasures the moment your work was over?

Of course you have known this was the wrong way to feel, and have been ashamed of it from the bottom of your heart, but still you have seen no way to help it. You have not *loved* your work, and, could you have done so with an easy conscience, you would have been glad to have given it up altogether.

Or, if this does not describe your case, perhaps another picture will. You do love your work in the abstract; but, in the doing of it, you find so many cares and responsibilities connected with it, so many misgivings and doubts as to your own capacity or fitness, that it becomes a very heavy burden, and you go to it bowed down and weary, before the labour has even begun. Then also you are continually distressing yourself about the results of your work, and greatly troubled if they are not just what you would like, and this of itself is a constant burden.

Now from all these forms of bondage the soul is entirely delivered that enters fully into the blessed life of faith. In the first place, service of any sort becomes delightful to it, because, having surrendered its will into the keeping of the Lord, He works in it to will and to do of His good pleasure, and the soul finds itself really *wanting* to do the things God wants it to do. It is always very pleasant to do the things we *want* to do, let them be ever so difficult of accomplishment, or involve ever so much of bodily weariness. If a man's *will* is really set on a thing, he regards with a sublime indifference the obstacles that lie in the way of his reaching it, and laughs to himself at the idea of any opposition or difficulties hindering him. How many men have gone gladly and thankfully to the ends of the world in search of worldly fortunes, or to fulfil worldly ambitions, and have scorned the thoughts of any cross connected with it! How many mothers have congratulated themselves and rejoiced over the honour done their sons in being promoted to some place of power and usefulness in their country's service, although it has involved perhaps years of separation, and a life of hardship for their dear ones! And yet these same men and these very mothers would have felt and said that they were taking up crosses too heavy almost to be borne, had the service of Christ required the same sacrifice of home, and friends, and worldly ease. It is altogether the way we look at things whether we think they are crosses or not. And I am ashamed to think that any Christian should ever put on a long face and shed tears over doing a thing for Christ, which a worldly man would be only too glad to do for money.

What we need in the Christian life is to get believers to *want* to do God's will as much as other people want to do their own will. And this is the idea of the Gospel. It is what God intended for us; and it is what He has promised. In describing the new covenant in Heb. 8:6-13, He says it shall no more be the old covenant made on Sinai—that is a law given from the outside, controlling a man by force—but it shall be a law written *within,* constraining a man by love. "I will put my laws," He says, "in their mind, and write them in their hearts." This can mean nothing but that we shall *love* His law, for anything written on our hearts we must love. And putting it into our minds is surely the game as God working in us to "will and to do of His good pleasure." and means that we shall will what God wills, and shall obey His sweet commands, not because it is our duty to do so, hut because we ourselves want to do what He wants us to do. Nothing could possibly be conceived more effectual than this. How often have we thought when dealing with our children, "Oh, if I could only get inside of them and make them *want* to do just what I want, how easy it would be to manage them then!" And how often practically in experience we have found that, to deal with cross-grained people, we must carefully avoid suggesting our wishes to them, but must in some way induce them to suggest them themselves, sure that then there will be no opposition to contend with. And we, who are by nature a stiff-necked people, always rebel more or less against a law from outside of us, while we joyfully embrace the same law springing up within.

God's plan for us therefore is to get possession of the inside of a man, to take the control and management of his will, and to work it for him; and then obedience is easy and a delight, and service becomes perfect freedom, until the Christian is forced to exclaim, "This happy service! Who could dream earth had such liberty?"

What you need to do then, dear Christian, if you are in bondage, is to put your will over completely into the hands of your Lord, surrendering to Him the entire control of it. Say, "Yes, Lord, YES!" to everything, and trust Him so to work in you to will, as to bring your whole wishes and affections into conformity with His own sweet, and lovable, and most lovely will. I have seen this done over and over, in cases where it looked beforehand an utterly impossible thing. In one case, where a lady had been for years rebelling fearfully against a thing which she knew was right, but which she hated, I saw her, out of the depths of despair and without any feeling, give her will in that matter up into the hands of her Lord, and begin to say to Him, "Thy will be done; *Thy will be done!*" And in one short hour that very thing began to look sweet and precious to her. It is wonderful what miracles God works in wills that are utterly surrendered to Him. He turns hard things into easy, and bitter things into sweet. It is not that He puts easy things in the place of the hard, but He actually changes the hard thing into an easy one. And this is salvation. It is grand. Do try it, you who are going about your daily Christian living as to a hard and weary task, and see if the blessed Jesus will not transform the very life you live now as a bondage, into the most delicious liberty!

Or again, if you do love His will in the abstract, but find the doing of it hard and burdensome, from this also there is deliverance in the wonderful life of faith. For in this life no burdens are carried, nor anxieties felt. The Lord is our burden bearer, and upon Him we must lay off every care. He says, in effect, "Be careful for nothing," but just make your requests known to Me, and I will attend to them all. Be careful for *nothing*, He says, not even your service. Above all, I should think, our service, because we know ourselves to be so utterly helpless in this, that even if we were careful it would not amount to anything. What have we to do with thinking whether we are fit or not! The Master-workman surely has a right to use any tool He pleases for His own work, and it is plainly not the business of the tool to decide whether it is the right one to be used or not. He knows, and if He chooses to use us, of course we must be fit. And in truth, if we only knew it, our chiefest fitness is in our utter helplessness. His strength can only be made perfect in our weakness. I can give you a splendid illustration of this.

I was once visiting an idiot asylum and looking at the children going through dumb-bell exercises. Now we all know that it is a very difficult thing for idiots to manage their movements. They have strength enough, generally, but no skill to use this strength, and as a consequence cannot do much. And in these dumb-bell exercises this deficiency was very apparent. They made all sorts of awkward movements. Now and then, by a happy chance, they would make a movement in harmony with the music, and the teacher's directions, but for the most part all was out of harmony. One little girl, however, I noticed, who made perfect movements. Not a jar nor a break disturbed the harmony of her exercises. And the reason was, not that she had more strength than the others, but that she had no strength at all. She could not so much as close her hands over the dumb-bells, nor lift her arms, and the master had to stand behind her and do it all. She yielded up her members as instruments to him, and his strength was made perfect in her weakness. He knew how to go through those exercises, for he himself had planned them, and therefore when he did it, it was done right. She did nothing but yield herself up utterly into his hands and he did it all. The yielding was her part, the responsibility was all his. It was not her skill that was needed to make harmonious movements, but only his. The question was not of her capacity, but of his. Her utter weakness was her greatest strength. And if this is a picture of our Christian life it is no wonder that Paul could say, "Most gladly therefore will I rather *glory* in my infirmities, that the power of Christ may rest upon me." Who would not glory in being so utterly weak and helpless, that the Lord Jesus Christ should find no hindrance to the perfect working of His mighty power through us and in us?

Then, too, if the work is His, the responsibility is His, and we have no room left for worrying about it. Everything in reference to it is known to Him, and He can manage it all. Why not leave it all with Him then, and consent to be treated like a child and guided where to go? It is a fact that the most effectual workers I know are those who do not feel the least care or anxiety about their work, but who commit it all to their dear Master, and, asking Him to guide them moment by moment in reference to it, trust Him implicitly for each moment's needed supplies of wisdom and of strength. To see such, you would almost think perhaps that they were too free from care, where such mighty interests are at stake. But when you have learned God's secret of trusting, and see the beauty and the power of that life which is yielded up to His working, you will cease to condemn, and will begin to wonder how any of God's workers can dare to carry burdens, or assume responsibilities which He alone is able to bear.

There are one or two other bonds of service from which this life of trust delivers us. We find out that we are not responsible for all the work in the world. The commands cease to be general, and become personal and individual. The Master does not map out a general course of action for us, and leave us to get along through it by our own wisdom and skill as best we may, but He leads us step by step, giving us each hour the especial guidance needed for that hour. His blessed Spirit dwelling in us, brings to our remembrance *at the time* the necessary command. So that we do not need to take any thought ahead, but simply to take each step as it is made known to us, following our Lord whithersoever He leads us. "The *steps* of a good man are ordered of the Lord," not his way only, but each separate step in that way. Many Christians make the mistake of expecting to receive God's commands all in a lump, as it were. They think because He tells them to give a tract to one person in a railway train, for instance, that He means them always to give tracts to everybody, and they burden themselves with an impossible command.

There was a young Christian once, who, because the Lord had sent her to speak a message to one soul whom she met in a walk, took it as a general command for always, and thought she must speak to every one she met about their souls. This was of course impossible, and as a consequence she was soon in hopeless bondage about it. She became absolutely afraid to go outside of her own door, and lived in perpetual condemnation. At last she disclosed her distress to a friend who was instructed in the ways of God with His servants, and this friend told her she was making a great mistake; that the Lord had His own especial work for each especial workman, and that the servants in a well-regulated household might as well each one take it upon themselves to try and do the work of all the rest, as for the Lord's servants to think they were each one under obligation to do everything. He told her just to put herself under the Lord's personal guidance as to her work, and trust Him to point out to her each particular person to whom He would have her speak, assuring her that He never puts forth His own sheep without going before them, and making a way for them Himself. She followed this advice, and laid the burden of her work on the Lord, and the result was a happy pathway of daily guidance, in which she was led into much blessed work for her Master, but was able to do it all without a care or a burden, because He led her out and prepared the way before her.

Putting ourselves into God's hands in this way, seems to me just like making the junction between the machinery and the steam-engine. The power is not in the machinery, but in the steam. Disconnected from the engine, the machinery is perfectly useless. But let the connection be made, and the machinery goes easily and without effort, because of the mighty power there is behind it. Thus the Christian life becomes an easy, natural life when it is the development of the Divine life working within. Most Christians live on a strain, because their wills are not fully in harmony with the will of God—the connection is not perfectly made at every point, and it requires an effort to move the machinery. But when once the connection is fully made, and the law of the Spirit of life in Christ Jesus can work in us with all its mighty power, we are then indeed made free from the law of sin and death, and shall know the glorious liberty of the children of God.

Another form of bondage as to service from which the life of faith delivers the soul, is in reference to the after-reflections which always follow any Christian work. These are always of one of two kinds. Either the soul congratulates itself upon its success, and is lifted up; or it is distressed over its failure, and is utterly cast down. One of these is *sure* to come, and of the two I think the first is the most to be dreaded, although the last causes at the time the greatest suffering. But in the life of trust neither will trouble us. For, having committed ourselves in our work to the Lord, we will be satisfied to leave it to Him, and will not think about ourselves in the matter at all.

Years ago I came across this sentence in an old book:—"Never indulge, at the close of an action, in any self-reflective acts of any kind, whether of self-congratulation or of self-despair. Forget the things that are behind the moment they are past, leaving them with God." It has been of unspeakable value to me. When the temptation comes, as it always does, to indulge in these reflections, either of one sort or the other, I turn from them at once and positively refuse to think about my work at all, leaving it with the Lord to overrule the mistakes, and to bless it as He chooses.

To sum it all up then, what is needed for happy and effectual service is simply to put your work into the Lord's hands, and leave it there. Do not take it to Him in prayer, saying, "Lord, guide me, Lord give me wisdom, Lord arrange for me," and then arise from your knees, and take the burden all back, and try to guide and arrange for yourself. *Leave* it with the Lord; and remember that what you trust to Him you must not worry over nor feel anxious about. Trust and worry cannot go together. If your work is a burden, it is because you are not trusting it to Him. But if you do trust it to Him, you will surely find that the yoke He puts upon you is easy, and the burden He gives you to carry is light, and even in the midst of a life of ceaseless activity you shall find rest to your soul.

If our dear Lord only had a band of such workers as this, there is no limit to what He might do with them. Truly, one such would "chase a thousand, and two would put ten thousand to flight," and nothing would be impossible to them. For it is nothing with the Lord "to help, whether with many, or with them that have no power."

May God raise up such an army speedily! And may you, my dear reader, enroll your name among this band of helpless, trusting ones, and, yielding yourself unto God as one who is alive from the dead, may every one of your members be also yielded unto Him as instruments of righteousness, to be used by Him as He pleases.

11

DIFFICULTIES CONCERNING GUIDANCE

YOU HAVE NOW BEGUN, dear reader, the life of faith. You have given yourself to the Lord to be His wholly and altogether, and He has taken you and has begun to mould and fashion you into a vessel unto His honour. Tour one most earnest desire is to be very pliable in His hands, and to follow Him whithersoever He may lead you, and you are trusting Him to work in you to will and to do of His good pleasure. But you find a great difficulty here. You have not learned yet to know the voice of the Good Shepherd, and are therefore in great doubt and perplexity as to what really is His will concerning you.

Perhaps there are certain paths into which God seems to be calling you, of which your friends utterly disapprove. And these friends, it may be, are older than yourself in the Christian life, and seem to you also to be much further advanced. You can scarcely bear to differ from them or distress them; and you feel also very diffident of yielding to any seeming impressions of duty of which they do not approve. And yet you cannot get rid of these impressions, and you are plunged into great doubt and uneasiness.

There is a way out of all these difficulties to the fully surrendered soul. I would repeat *fully* surrendered, because if there is any reserve of will upon any point, it becomes almost impossible to find out the mind of God in reference to that point; and therefore the first thing is to be sure that you really do *purpose* to obey the Lord in every respect. If however this is the case, and your soul only needs to know the will of God in order to consent to it, then you surely cannot doubt His willingness to make His will known, and to guide you in the right paths. There are many very clear promises in reference to this. Take, for instance, John 10:3, 4, "He calleth His own sheep by name, and leadeth them out. And when He putteth forth His own sheep He goeth before them, and the sheep follow Him, for they know His voice." Or, John 14:26: "But the Comforter, which is the Holy Ghost, whom the Father will send in my name, He shall teach you all things, and bring all things to your remembrance, whatsoever I have said unto you." Or, James 1:5, 6: "If any of you lack wisdom, let Him ask of God, that giveth to all men liberally, and upbraideth not; and it shall be given him." With such passages as these, and many more like them, we must believe that Divine guidance is promised to us, and our faith must confidently look for and expect it. This is essential, for in James 1:6, 7, we are told, "Let him ask in faith nothing wavering. For he that wavereth is like a wave of the sea, driven with the wind and tossed. For let not such a man think that he shall receive anything of the Lord."

Settle this point then first of all, that Divine guidance has been promised, and that you are sure to have it, if you ask for it; and let no suggestion of doubt turn you from this.

Next, you must remember that our God has all knowledge and all wisdom, and that therefore it is very possible He may guide you into paths wherein *He* knows great blessings are awaiting you, but which to the short-sighted human eyes around you seem sure to result in confusion and loss. You must recognise the fact that God's thoughts are not as man's thoughts, nor His ways as man's ways; and that He who knows the end of things from the beginning alone can judge of what the results of any course of action may be. You must therefore realise that His very love for you may perhaps lead you to run counter to the loving wishes of even your dearest friends. You must learn from Luke 14:26-33, and similar passages, that in order—not, to be saved but,—to be a disciple or follower of your Lord, you may perhaps be called upon to forsake all that you have, and to turn your backs on even father or mother, or brother or sister, or husband or wife, or it may be your own life also. Unless the possibility of this is clearly recognised, the soul will be very likely to get into difficulty, because it often happens that the child of God who enters upon this life-obedience is sooner or later led into paths which meet with the disapproval of those he best loves; and unless he is prepared for this, and can trust the Lord through it all, he will scarcely know what to do.

All this, it will of course be understood, is perfectly in harmony with those duties of honour and love which we owe to one another in the various relations of life. The nearer we are to Christ, the more shall we be enabled to exemplify the meekness and gentleness of our Lord, and the more tender will be our consideration for those who are our natural guardians and counsellors. The Saviour's guidance will always manifest itself by the Saviour's Spirit, and where, in obedience to Christ, we are led to act contrary to the advice or wishes of our friends, we shall prove that this i» our motive, by the love and patience which will mark our conduct.

But this point having been settled, we come now to the question as to how God's guidance is to come to us, and how we shall be able to know His voice.

There are two especial ways in which He reveals His will to us— through the Scriptures, and by means of the direct voice of His Holy Spirit, making impressions upon our hearts and our judgments.

The first of these is the guidance to be found in the Bible. Until you have found and obeyed God's will in reference to any subject as it is there revealed, you need not ask nor expect a separate direct personal revelation. A great many fatal mistakes are made in this matter of guidance, by the overlooking of this simple rule. Where our Father has written out for us a plain direction about anything He will not of course make an especial revelation to us about that thing. And if we fail to search out and obey the Scripture rule, where there is one, and look instead for an inward voice, we shall open ourselves to the deceptions of Satan, and shall almost inevitably get into error. No man, for instance, needs or could expect any direct revelation to tell him not to steal, because God has already in the Scriptures plainly declared His will about it. This seems such an obvious thing that I would not speak of it, but that I have frequently met with Christians who have altogether overlooked it, and have gone off into fanaticism as the result. I know the Bible does not always give a rule for every particular course of action, and in these cases we need and must expect the direct voice of the Spirit.

And yet the Scriptures are far more explicit even about details than most people think. And there are not many important affairs in life for which a clear direction may not be found in God's book. Take the matter of dress, and we have 1 Pet. 3:3, 4, and 1 Tim. 2:9. Take the matter of conversation, and we have Eph. 4:29, and 5:4. Take the matter of avenging injuries and standing up for your rights, and we have Rom. 12:19, 20, 21, and Matt. 5:38-48, and 1 Pet. 2:19-21. Take the matter of forgiving one another, and we have Eph. 4:32, and Mark 11:25, 26. Take the matter of conformity to the world, and we have Rom. 12:2, and 1 John 2:15-17, and James 4:4. Take the matter of anxieties of all kind, and we have Matt. 6:25-34, and Phil. 4:6, 7.

I only give these as examples to show how very full and practical the Bible guidance is. If, therefore, you find yourself in perplexity, first of all search arid see whether the Bible speaks on the point in question, asking God to make plain to you by the power of His Spirit, through the Scriptures, what is His mind. And whatever shall seem to you to be plainly taught there, that you must obey.

When we read and meditate upon this record of God's mind and will, with our understandings thus illuminated by the inspiring Spirit, our obedience will be as truly an obedience to a present, living word, as though it were afresh spoken to us to-day by our Lord from Heaven. The Bible is not only an ancient message from God sent to us many ages ago, but it is a present message sent to us each time we read it. "The words that I speak unto you, they are spirit, and they are life," and obedience to these words now is a living obedience to a present and personal command.

Especial guidance, therefore, superseding that of the Scriptures on any point about which the Scriptures are explicit, is not to be looked for; and no guidance of the Spirit can ever be contrary to Scripture.

But if, upon searching, you do not find in the Bible any directions upon your point of difficulty, or if the directions given do not reach into all the especial details of the case, then you have a right to ask and to expect direct guidance by the voice of the Spirit, speaking in your soul, and making distinct impressions upon your mind as to your duty. He will surely guide you into the right paths, and will make known to you God's sweet will concerning you; and you may realise not only your way, but even your very *steps* to be ordered by Him.

But in giving yourselves up to these impressions of duty, there are two points very important to guard. If they are from the Spirit they will be in accordance with Scripture and with a sanctified judgment, for God has surely not revealed His will in one place to contradict it in another, and His direct promise is that the "meek He will guide in judgment." Anything therefore which is contrary to Scripture or to a sanctified judgment must be rejected as from Satan. For we must never forget that Satan can make impressions upon our minds as well as the blessed Spirit of God, and in this matter of guidance it is especially necessary not to be ignorant of his devices. Sometimes, under a mistaken idea of exalting the Divine Spirit, earnest and honest Christians have ignored and even violated the teachings of Scripture, and have outraged their judgments. God, who sees the sincerity of their hearts, can and does pity and forgive, but the consequences as to this life are often very sad. In nothings therefore do we so much need to realise our own helplessness and to cast ourselves in child-like trust on the Lord, telling Him our danger of being deceived and trusting Him not to permit it. Every peculiarly precious spiritual gift is always necessarily linked with some peculiar danger, and this supreme blessing of direct guidance is no exception to this rule. But with the tests I have mentioned, and with an absolute committing of the whole matter to the Lord, and a perfect confidence in Him, there is nothing to fear.

And now I have guarded the points of danger, do permit me to let myself out for a little to the blessedness and joy of this direct communication of God's will to us. It seems to me to be the grandest of privileges. In the first place, that God should love me enough to *care* about the details of my life is perfectly wonderful. And then that He should be willing to tell me all about it, and to let me know just how to live and walk so as to perfectly please Him, seems almost too good to be true. We never care about the little details of people's lives unless we love them. It is a matter of indifference to us with the majority of people we meet as to what they do or how they spend their time. But as soon as we begin to love any one, we begin at once to care. That God cares, therefore, is just a precious proof of His love; and it is most blessed to have Him speak to us about everything in our lives—about our dress— about our reading—about our friendships—about our occupations— about all that we do, or think, or say. You *must* know this in your own experience, dear reader, if you would come into the full joy and privilege of this life hid with Christ in God, for it is one of its most precious gifts!

God's promise is, that He will work in us to *will* as well as to do of His good pleasure. This of course means that He will take possession of our will and work it for us, and that His suggestions will come to us, not so much commands from the outside, as desires springing up within. They will originate in our will; we shall feel as though we *wanted* to do so and so, not as though we *must*. And this makes it a service of perfect liberty; for it is always easy to do what we desire to do, let the accompanying circumstances be as difficult as they may. Every mother knows that she could secure perfect and easy obedience in her child, if she could only get into that child's will and work it for him, making him want himself to do the things she willed he should. And this is what our Father does for His children in the new dispensation,—He writes His laws on our hearts and on our minds, and we love them, and are drawn to our obedience by our affections and judgment, not driven by our fears.

The way in which the Holy Spirit, therefore, usually works in this direct guidance is to impress upon the mind a wish or desire to do or to leave undone certain things.

The soul when engaged, perhaps, in prayer, feels a sudden suggestion made to its inmost consciousness in reference to a certain point of duty. "I would like to do this or the other," it thinks "I wish I could." Or perhaps the suggestion may come as a question, "I wonder whether I ought not to do so and so?" Or it may be only at first in the way of a conviction that such is the right and best thing to be done.

At once the matter should be committed to the Lord, with an instant consent of the will to obey Him; and if the suggestion is in accordance with the Scriptures and a sanctified judgment, and it continues to seem right, an immediate obedience is the safest and easiest course. At the moment when the Spirit speaks, it is always easy to obey; if the soul hesitates and begins to reason, it becomes more and more difficult continually. As a general rule the first impressions are the right ones in a fully-surrendered heart, for God is faithful in His dealings with us, and will cause His voice to be heard before any other voices. Such impressions, therefore, should never be met by reasoning. Prayer and trust are the only safe attitudes of the soul, and even these should be but momentary, as it were, lest the time for action should pass, and the blessing be missed.

If, however, the suggestion does not seem quite clear enough to act upon, and doubt and perplexity ensue, especially if it is something about which one's friends differ from us, then we may need, perhaps, a time of waiting on the Lord for further light. But we must wait in faith, and in an attitude of entire surrender, saying "Yes!" continually to the will of our Lord, let it be what it may. If the suggestion is from Him, it will continue and strengthen; if it is not from Him, it will disappear, and we shall forget we ever had it. If it continues,—if every time we are brought into near communion with the Lord it seems to return, —if it troubles us in our moments of prayer, and disturbs all our peace, we may then feel sure it is from God, and we must yield to it or suffer an unspeakable loss.

I believe myself the only safe way is always to yield up the doubtful things to God, until we have clear light to take them back.

A dear lady, who had walked in a life of consecration for many years, told me that her invariable rule was to decide every doubtful matter on the self-denying side, and that she had never once had occasion to regret it. It was the secret of a life of wonderful devotedness. The Apostle gives us a rule in reference to doubtful things, which seems to me very explicit. He is speaking about certain kinds of meat-eating which were ceremonially unclean, and, after declaring his own liberty, says,—"I know and am persuaded by the Lord Jesus, that there is nothing unclean of itself. But to him that esteemeth anything unclean, to him it is unclean." And in summing up the whole subject, he writes:— "Hast thou faith? have it to thyself before God. Happy is he that condemneth not himself in that thing which he alloweth. And he that doubteth is damned (condemned) if he eat, because he eateth not of faith: for whatsoever is not of faith is sin." The doubtful things must all be surrendered, dear Christian, until God gives you light to know more clearly His mind concerning them. And as a general thing you will find that the very doubt has been His voice calling upon you to come into a more perfect conformity to His will.

Take all your present perplexities, then, to Jesus. Tell Him you only want to know and obey His voice, and ask Him to make it plain to you. Promise Him that you will obey, whatever it may be. Believe implicitly that He is guiding you, according to His word. Surrender all the doubtful things until you have clearer light Look and listen for His dear voice continually, and the moment you are sure of it yield an immediate obedience. Trust Him to make you forget the impression if it is not His will, and if it continues, believe that He is faithful and would not let you be deceived.

Above everything else trust Him. Nowhere is faith more needed than here. He has promised to guide. You have asked Him to do it, And now you must believe that He does, and must take what comes as being His guidance. No earthly parent or master could guide his children or servants if they should refuse to take his commands as being really the expression of his will. And God cannot guide those souls who never trust Him enough to believe that He is doing it

And oh, do not be afraid of this sweet life, lived hour by hour and day by day under the guidance of thy Lord! If He seeks to bring thee out of the world and into a very close conformity to Himself, do not shrink from it. It is thy most blessed privilege. Rejoice in it. Embrace it eagerly. Let everything go that it may be thine.

"Dole not thy duties out to God,
But let thy hand be free:
Look long at Jesus; His sweet blood
How was it dealt to thee?

"The perfect way is hard to flesh;
It is not hard to love;
If thou wert sick for want of God,
How swiftly would'st thou *move*!

"Then keep thy conscience sensitive;
No inward token miss:
And go where grace entices thee; —
Perfection lies in this."

12

CONCERNING TEMPTATION

ERTAIN VERY GREAT MISTAKES are made concerning this matter of temptation, in the practical working out of this life of faith.

First of all, people seem to expect that, after the soul has entered into its rest in Jesus, temptations will cease, and to think that the promised deliverance is not only to be from yielding to temptation, but even also from being tempted. Consequently, when they find the Canaanite still in the land, and see the cities great and walled-up to Heaven, they are utterly discouraged, and think they must have gone wrong in some way, and that this cannot be the true land after all.

Then next they make the mistake of looking upon temptation as sin, and of blaming themselves for what in reality is the fault of Satan only. This brings them into condemnation and discouragement; and discouragement, if continued in, always ends at last in actual sin. Satan makes an easy prey of a discouraged soul. So that we fall often from the very fear of having fallen.

To meet the first of these difficulties, it is only necessary to refer to the Scripture declarations, that the Christian life is to be throughout a warfare; and that, especially when seated in heavenly places in Christ Jesus, we are to wrestle against spiritual enemies there, whose power and skill to tempt us must doubtless be far superior to any we have ever heretofore encountered. As a fact, temptations generally increase in strength tenfold after we have entered into the interior life, rather than decrease. And no amount or sort of them must ever for a moment lead us to suppose we have not really found the true abiding place. Strong temptations are generally a sign of great grace, rather than of little grace. When the Children of Israel had first left Egypt, the Lord did not lead them through the country of the Philistines, although that was the nearest way; "for God said, lest peradventure the people repent when they see war, and they return to Egypt." But afterwards, when they had learned better how to trust Him, He permitted their enemies to attack them. Then also in their wilderness journey they met with but few enemies, and fought but few battles compared to those in the land, where they found seven great nations, and thirty-one kings to be conquered, besides walled cities to be taken, and giants to be overcome.

They could not have fought with the Canaanites, and the Hittites, and the Amorites, and the Perizzites, and the Hivites, and the Jebusites, until they had gone into the land where these enemies were. And the very power of your temptations, dear Christian, therefore, may perhaps be one of the strongest proofs that you really are in the land you have been seeking to enter, because they are temptations peculiar to that land. You must never allow them to cause you to question the fact of your having entered it.

The second mistake is not quite so easy to deal with. It seems hardly worth while to say that temptation is not sin, and yet most of the distress about it arises from not understanding this fact. The very suggestion of wrong seems to bring pollution with it, and, Satan's agency not being recognised, the poor tempted soul begins to feel as if it must be very bad indeed, and very far off from God, to have had such thoughts and suggestions. It is as though a burglar should break into a man's house to steal, and, when the master of the house began to resist him and drive him out, should turn round and accuse the owner of being himself the thief. It is Satan's grand ruse for entrapping us. He comes and whispers suggestions of evil to us,—doubts, blasphemies, jealousies, envyings, and pride,—and then turns round and says, "Oh, how wicked you must be to think of such things! It is very plain that you are not trusting the Lord; for if you were it would have been impossible for these things to have entered your heart." His reasoning sounds so very plausible that the soul often accepts it as true, and at once comes under condemnation, and is filled with discouragement. Then it is easy for Satan to lead it on into actual sin. One of the most fatal things in the life of faith is discouragement. One of the most helpful is cheerfulness. A very wise man once said that in overcoming temptations cheerfulness was the first thing, cheerfulness the second, and cheerfulness the third. We must *expect* to conquer. That is why the Lord said so often to Joshua, "Be strong and of a good courage;" "Be not afraid, neither be thou dismayed;" "Only be thou strong and very courageous." And it is also the reason He says to us, "Let not your heart be troubled, neither let it be afraid." The power of temptation is in the fainting of our own hearts. Satan knows this well, and he always begins his assaults by discourging us, if he can in any way accomplish it.

Sometimes this discouragement arises from what we think is a righteous grief and disgust at ourselves that such things *could* be any temptation to us; but which is really a mortification arising from the fact that we have been indulging in a secret self-congratulation that our tastes were too pure, or our separation from the world was too complete for such things to tempt us. We have expected something from ourselves, and have been sorely disappointed not to find that something there, and are discouraged in consequence. This mortification and discouragement are really a far worse condition than the temptation itself, though they present an appearance of true humility, for they are nothing but the results of wounded self-love. True humility can bear to see its own utter weakness and foolishness revealed, because it never expected anything from itself, and knows that its only hope and expectation must be in God. Therefore, instead of discouraging the soul from trusting, it drives it to a deeper and more utter trust. But the counterfeit humility which Satan produces plunges the soul into the depths of a faithless discouragement, and drives it into the very sin at which it is so distressed.

I remember once hearing an allegory that illustrated this to me wonderfully. Satan called together a council of his servants to consult how they might make a good man sin. One evil spirit started up and said, "I will make him sin." "How will you do it?" asked Satan. "I will set before him the pleasures of sin," was the reply; "I will tell him of its delights, and the rich rewards it brings." "Ah," said Satan, "that will not do; he has tried it, and knows better than that." Then another spirit started up and said, "I will make him sin." "What will you do asked

Satan?" "I will tell him of the pains and sorrows of virtue. I will show him that virtue has no delights, and brings no rewards." "Ah, no!" exclaimed Satan, "that will not do at all; for he has tried it, and knows that 'wisdom's ways *are* ways of pleasantness, and all her paths are peace.'" "Well," said another imp, starting up, "I will undertake to make him sin." "And what will you do?" asked Satan again. "I will discourage his soul," was the short reply. "Ah, that will do!" cried Satan, "that will do! We shall conquer him now." And they did.

An old writer says, "All discouragement is from the devil;" and I wish every Christian would just take this as a pocket-piece, and never forget it. We must fly from discouragement as we would from sin.

But this is impossible if we fail to recognise Satan's agency in temptation; for, if the temptations are our own fault, we cannot help being discouraged. But they are not. The Bible says, "Blessed is the man that endureth temptation;" and we are exhorted to "count it all joy when we fall into divers temptations." Temptation, therefore, cannot be sin; and the truth is, it is no more a sin to hear these whispers and suggestions of Satan in our souls than it is for us to hear the swearing or wicked talk of bad men as we pass along the street. The sin only comes, in either case, by our stopping and joining in with them. If, when the wicked suggestions come, we turn from them at once, as we would from wicked talk, and pay no more attention to them, we do not sin. But, if we carry them on in our minds, and roll them under our tongues, and dwell on them with a half-consent of our will to them as true, then we sin. We may be enticed by Satan a thousand times a-day without sin; and we cannot help his enticings. But, if he can succeed in making us think that *his* enticings are *our* sin, he has accomplished half the battle, and can hardly fail to gain a complete victory.

A dear lady once came to me under great darkness, simply from not understanding this. She had been living very happily in the life of faith for some time, and had been so free from temptation as almost to begin to think she would never be tempted any more. But suddenly a very peculiar form of temptation had assailed her, which had horrified her. She found that, the moment she began to pray, dreadful thoughts of all kinds would rush into her mind. She had lived a very sheltered, innocent life, and these thoughts seemed so awful to her that she felt she must be one of the most wicked of sinners to be capable of having them. She began by thinking she could not possibly have entered into the rest of faith, and ended by concluding that she had never even been born again. Her soul was in an agony of distress. I told her that these dreadful thoughts were altogether the suggestions of Satan, who came to her the moment she knelt in prayer, and poured them into her mind, and that she herself was not to blame for them at all; that she could not help them any more than she could help hearing if a wicked man should pour out his blasphemies in her presence. And I urged her to recognise and treat them as from Satan; not to blame herself or be discouraged, but to turn at once to Jesus, and commit them to Him. I showed her how great an advantage Satan had gained by making her think these thoughts were originated by herself, and plunging her into condemnation and discouragement on account of them. And I assured her she would find a speedy victory if she would pay no attention to them; but, ignoring their presence, would simply turn her back on them, and look to the Lord. She grasped the truth, and the next time these thoughts came she said to Satan, "I have found you out now. It is you who are suggesting these dreadful thoughts to me, and I hate them, and will have nothing to do with them. The Lord is my helper; take them to Him, and settle them in His presence." Immediately the baffled enemy, finding himself discovered, fled in confusion, and her soul was perfectly delivered.

Another thing also. Satan knows that if a Christian recognises a suggestion of evil as coming from him, he will recoil from it far more quickly than if it seems to be the suggestion of his own mind. If Satan prefaced each temptation with the words, "I am Satan, your relentless enemy; I have come to make you sin," I suppose we would hardly feel any desire at all to yield to his suggestions. He has to hide himself in order to make his baits attractive. And our victory will be far more easily gained if we are not ignorant of his devices, but recognise him at his very first approach.

We also make another great mistake about temptations in thinking that all time spent in combating them is lost. Hours pass, and we seem to have made no progress, because we have been so beset with temptations. But it often happens that we have been serving God far more truly during these hours, than in our times of comparative freedom from temptation. Temptation is really more the devil's wrath against God than against us. He cannot touch our Saviour, but he can wound our Saviour by conquering us, and our ruin is important to him only as it affects Him. "We are, therefore, really fighting our Lord's battles when we are fighting temptation, and hours are often worth days to us under these circumstances. "We read, "Blessed is the man that *endureth* temptation," and I am sure this means enduring the continuance of it and its frequent recurrence. Nothing so cultivates the grace of patience as the endurance of temptation, and nothing so drives the soul to an utter dependence upon the Lord Jesus as its continuance. And finally, nothing brings more praise and honour and glory to our dearest Lord Himself than the trial of our faith .which comes through manifold temptations. "We are told that it is more precious than gold, though it be tried with fire, and that we, who patiently endure the trial, shall receive for our reward "the crown of life which the Lord hath promised to them that love Him."

We cannot wonder, therefore, any longer at the exhortation with which the Holy Ghost opens the book of James: "Count it all joy when ye fall into divers temptations, knowing this, that the trying of your faith worketh patience. But let patience have her perfect work, that ye may be perfect and entire, wanting nothing."

Temptation is plainly to be the blessed instrument used by God to complete our perfection, and thus Satan's own weapons are turned against himself, and we see how it is that all things, even temptations, can work together for good to them that love God.

As to the way of victory over temptations, it seems hardly necessary to say to those whom I am at this time especially addressing, that it is to be by faith. For this is, of course, the foundation upon which the whole interior life rests. Our one great motto is throughout, "We are nothing,

100

Christ is all." And always and everywhere we have started out to stand, and walk, and overcome, and live by faith. We have discovered our own utter helplessness, and know that we cannot do anything for ourselves. Our only way, therefore, is to hand the temptation over to our Lord, and trust Him to conquer it for us. But when we put it into His hands we must *leave* it there. It must be as real a committing of ourselves to Him for victory, as it was at first a committing of ourselves to Him for salvation. He must do all for us in the one case as completely as in the other. It was faith only then, and it must be faith only now.

And the victories which the Lord works in conquering the temptations of those who thus trust Him are nothing short of miracles, as thousands can testify.

But into this part of the subject I cannot go at present, as my object has been rather to present temptation in its true light than to develop the way of victory over it. I want to deliver conscientious faithful souls from the bondage into which they are sure to be brought, if they fail to understand the true nature and use of temptation, and confound it with sin. I want that they should not be ignorant of Satan's devices, but that, recognising his agency in all their temptations, they should be able to say at once, "Get thee behind me;" and should walk even through the midst of the fiercest assaults with unclouded and triumphant peace, knowing that "when the enemy shall come in like a flood, the Spirit of the Lord shall lift up a standard against him."

13

FAILURES

T HE VERY TITLE OF THIS chapter may perhaps startle some. "Failures," they will say; "we thought there were no failures in this life of faith!"

To this I would answer that there ought not to be, and need not be; but, as a fact, there sometimes are. And we have got to deal with facts, and not with theories. No teacher of this interior life ever says that it becomes impossible to sin; they only insist that sin ceases to be a necessity, and that a possibility of uniform victory is opened before us. And there are very few who do not confess that as to their own actual experience they have at times been overcome by momentary temptation.

Of course, in speaking of sin here, I mean conscious, known sin. I do not touch on the subject of sins of ignorance, or what is called the inevitable sin of our nature, which are all covered by the Atonement, and do not disturb our fellowship with God. I have no desire nor ability to treat of the doctrines concerning sin,—these I will leave with the theologians to discuss and settle, while I speak only of the believer's experience in the matter. And I wish it to be fully understood that in all I shall say I have reference simply to that which comes within the range of our consciousness.

Misunderstanding, then, on this point of known or conscious sin, opens the way for great dangers in the higher Christian life. When a believer, who has, as he trusts, entered upon the highway of holiness, finds himself surprised into sin, he is tempted either to be utterly discouraged, and to give everything up as lost; or else, in order to preserve the doctrine untouched, he feels it necessary to cover his sin up, calling it infirmity, and refusing to be honest and above-board about it. Either of these courses is equally fatal to any real growth and progress in the life of holiness. The only way is to face the sad fact at once, call the thing by its right name, and discover, if possible, the reason and the remedy. This life of union with God requires the utmost honesty with Him and with ourselves. The blessing which the sin itself would only momentarily disturb, is sure to be lost by any dishonest dealing with it. A sudden failure is no reason for being discouraged and giving up all as lost. Neither is the integrity of our doctrine touched by it. We are not preaching a *state*, but a *walk*. The highway of holiness is not a *place*, but a *way*. Sanctification is not a thing to be picked up at a certain stage of our experience, and for ever after possessed, but it is a life to be lived day by day, and hour by hour. We may for a moment turn aside from a path, but the path is not obliterated by our wandering, and can be instantly regained. And in this life and walk of faith, there may be momentary failures which, although very sad and greatly to be deplored, need not, if rightly met, disturb the attitude of the soul as to entire consecration and perfect trust, nor interrupt, for more than the passing moment, its happy communion with its Lord.

The great point is an instant return to God. Our sin is no reason for ceasing to trust, but only an unanswerable argument why we must trust more fully than ever. From whatever cause we have been betrayed into failure, it is very certain that there is no remedy to be found for it in discouragement. As well might a child who is learning to walk, lie down in despair when he has fallen, and refuse to take another step, as a believer, who is seeking to learn how to live and walk by faith, give up in despair because of having fallen into sin. The only way in both cases is to get right up and try again. When the Children of Israel had met with that disastrous defeat, soon after their entrance into the land, before the little city of Ai, they were all so utterly discouraged that we read: "Wherefore the hearts of the people melted, and became as water. And Joshua rent his clothes, and fell to the earth upon his face before the ark of the Lord until the eventide, he and the elders of Israel, and put dust upon their heads. And Joshua said, 'Alas! O Lord God, wherefore hast Thou at all brought this people over Jordan to deliver us into the hands of the Amorites to destroy us? Would to God we had been content, and dwelt on the other side Jordan! O Lord, what shall I say, when Israel turneth their hacks before their enemies? For the Canaanites and all the inhabitants of the land shall hear of it, and shall environ us round and cut off our name from the earth: and what wilt Thou do unto Thy great name?"' What a wail of despair this was! And how exactly it is repeated by many a child of God in the present day, whose heart, because of a defeat, melts and becomes as water, and who cries out, "Would to God we had been content and dwelt on the other side Jordan!" and predicts for itself further failures and even utter discomfiture before its enemies. No doubt Joshua thought then, as we are apt to think now, that discouragement and despair were the only proper and safe condition after such a failure. But God thought otherwise. "And the Lord said unto Joshua, Get thee up; wherefore liest thou upon thy face?"

The proper thing to do, was not to abandon themselves thus to utter discouragement, humble as it might look, but at once to face the evil and get rid of it, and afresh and immediately to "sanctify themselves." "Up, sanctify the people," is always God's command. "Lie down and be discouraged," is always Satan's temptation. Our feeling is that it is presumptuous, and even almost impertinent, to go at once to the Lord after having sinned against Him. It seems as if we ought to suffer the consequences of our sin first for a little while, and endure the accusings of our conscience. And we can hardly believe that the Lord *can* be willing at once to receive us back into loving fellowship with Himself.

A little girl once expressed the feeling to me, with a child's outspoken candour. She had asked whether the Lord Jesus always forgave us for our sins as soon as we asked Him, and I had said "Yes, of course He does." *"Just* as soon?" she repeated, doubtingly. "Yes," I replied, "the very minute wo ask, He forgives us." "Well," she said deliberately, "I cannot believe that. I should think He would make us feel sorry for two or three days first. And then I should think He would make us ask Him a great many times, and in a very pretty way too,—not just in common talk. And I believe that *is* the way He does, and you need not try to make me think He forgives me right at once, no matter what the Bible says." She only *said* what most Christians *think*. And, what is worse, what most Christians act on, making their discouragement and their very remorse separate them infinitely further

104

off from God, than their sin would have done. Yet it is so totally contrary to the way we like our children to act towards us, that I wonder how we ever could have conceived such an idea of God. How a mother grieves when a naughty child goes off alone in despairing remorse, and doubts her willingness to forgive; and how, on the other hand, her whole heart goes out in welcoming love to the darling who runs to her at once and begs her forgiveness. Surely our God knew this yearning love when He said to us, "Return, ye backsliding children, and I will heal your backslidings."

The fact is, that the same moment which brings the consciousness of having sinned ought to bring also the consciousness of being forgiven. This is especially essential to an unwavering walk in the highway of holiness, for no separation from God can be tolerated here for an instant.

We can only walk in this path by looking continually unto Jesus, moment by moment; and if our eyes, are taken off of Him to look upon our own sin and our own weakness, we shall leave the path at once. The believer, therefore, who has, as he trusts, entered upon this highway, if he finds himself overcome by sin, must flee with it instantly to Jesus. He must act on 1 John 1:9: "If we confess our sins, He is faithful and just to forgive us our sins, and to cleanse us from all unrighteousness." He must not hide his sin and seek to salve it over with excuses, or to push it out of his memory by the lapse of time. But ho must do as the Children of Israel did, rise up *"early* in the morning," and *"run"* to the place where the evil thing is hidden, and take it out of its hiding place, and lay it "out before the Lord." He must confess his sin. And then he must stone it with stones, and burn it with fire, and utterly put it away from him, and raise over it a great heap of stones, that it may be for ever hidden from his sight. And he must believe then and there that God *is,* according to His word, faithful and just to forgive him his sin, and that He does do it; and further, that He also cleanses him from all unrighteousness. He must claim an immediate forgiveness and an immediate cleansing by faith, and must go on trusting harder and more absolutely than ever.

As soon as Israel's sin had been brought to light and put away, at once God's word came again in a message of glorious encouragement, "Fear not, neither be thou dismayed. . . . See, I have given into thy hand the king of Ai, and his people, and his city, and his land." Our courage must rise higher than ever, and we must abandon ourselves more completely to the Lord, that His mighty power may the more perfectly work in us all the good pleasure of His will. Moreover, we must forget our sin as soon as it is thus confessed and forgiven. We must not dwell on it, and examine it, and indulge in a luxury of distress and remorse. We must not put it on a pedestal, and then walk around it and view it on every side, and so magnify it into a mountain that hides our God from our eyes. We must follow the example of Paul, and "forgetting those things which are behind, and reaching forth unto those things which are before," we must "press toward the mark for the prize of the high calling of God in Christ Jesus."

I would like to bring up two contrastive illustrations of these things. One was an earnest Christian man, an active worker in the Church, who had been living for several months in the enjoyment of full salvation. He was suddenly overcome by a temptation to treat a brother unkindly. Not having supposed it possible that he could ever sin again, he was at once plunged into the deepest discouragement, and concluded he had been altogether mistaken, and had never entered into the life of full trust at all. Day by day his discouragement increased until it became despair, and he concluded he had never even been born again, and gave himself up for lost. He spent three years of utter misery, going further and further away from God, and being gradually drawn off into one sin after another, until his life was a curse to himself and to all around him. His health failed under the terrible burden, and fears were entertained for his reason. At the end of three years he met a Christian lady, who understood the truth about sin that I have been trying to explain. In a few moments conversation she found out his trouble, and at once said, "You sinned in that act, there is no doubt about it, and I do not want you to try and excuse it. But have you never confessed it to the Lord and asked Him to forgive you?" "Confess it!" he exclaimed, "why it

106

seems to me I have done nothing but confess it, and entreat God to forgive me night and day for all this three dreadful years." "And you have never believed He did forgive you?" asked the lady. "*No,*" said the poor man, how could I, for I never felt as if He did?" But suppose He had said He forgave you, would not that have done as well as for you to feel it?" "Oh, yes," replied the man, "if God said it, of course I would believe it." "Very well, He does say so," was the lady's answer, and she turned to the verse we have taken above (1 John 1:9) and read it aloud. "Now," she continued, "you have been all these three years confessing and confessing your sin, and all the while God's record has been declaring that He was faithful and just to forgive it and to cleanse you, and yet you have never once believed it. You have been 'making God a liar' all this while by refusing to believe His record."

The poor man saw the whole thing, and was dumb with amazement and consternation; and when the lady proposed they should kneel down, and that he should confess his past unbelief and sin, and should claim, then and there, a present forgiveness and a present cleansing, he obeyed like one in a maze. But the result was glorious. In a few moments the light broke in, and he burst out into praise at the wonderful deliverance. In three minutes his soul was enabled to traverse back by faith the whole long weary journey that he had been three years in making, and he found himself once more resting in Jesus, and rejoicing in the fulness of His salvation.

The other illustration was the case of a Christian lady who had been living in the land of promise about two weeks, and who had had a very bright and victorious experience. Suddenly, at the end of that time, she was overcome by a violent burst of anger. For a moment a flood of discouragement swept over her soul. Satan said, "There, now, that shows it was all a mistake. Of course you have been deceived about the whole thing, and have never entered into the life of full trust at all. And now you may as well give up altogether, for you never can consecrate yourself any more entirely, nor trust any more fully, than you did this time; so it is very plain this life of holiness is not for you!" These thoughts flashed through her mind in a moment, but she was well taught in the ways of God, and she said at once, "Yes, I have sinned, and it is very sad. But the Bible says that if we confess our sins, God is faithful and just to forgive us our sins and to cleanse us from all unrighteousness, and I believe He will do it." She did not delay a moment, but while still boiling over with anger, she ran—she could not walk—into a room where she could be alone, and kneeling down beside the bed, she said, "Lord, I confess my sin. I have sinned, I am even at this very moment sinning. I hate it, but I cannot get rid of it. I confess it with shame and confusion of face to Thee. And now I believe that, according to Thy word, Thou dost forgive and Thou dost cleanse." She said it out loud, for the inward turmoil was too great for it to be said inside. As the words "Thou dost forgive and Thou dost cleanse" passed her lips, the deliverance came. The Lord said, "Peace, be still," and there was a great calm. A flood of light and joy burst on her soul, the enemy fled, and she was more than conqueror through Him that loved her. The whole thing—the sin and the recovery from it—had occupied not five minutes, and her feet trod on more firmly than ever in the blessed highway of holiness. Thus the valley of Achor became to her a door of hope, and she sang afresh and with deeper meaning her song of deliverance, "I will sing unto the Lord, for He hath triumphed; gloriously."

The truth is, the only remedy after all in every emergency is to trust in the Lord. And if this is all we ought to do, and all we can do, is it not better to do it at once? I have often been brought up short by the question, "Well, what can I do but trust?" And I have realised at once the folly of seeking for deliverance in any other way, by saying to myself, "I shall have to come to simple trusting in the end, and why not come to it at once, now in the beginning." It is a life and walk of *faith* we have entered upon, and if we fail in it, our only recovery must lie in an increase of faith, not in a lessening of it.

Let every failure, then, if any occur, drive you; instantly to Jesus with a more complete abandonment and a more perfect trust, and you will find that, sad as they are, they will not take you out of the land of rest, nor permanently interrupt your sweet communion with Him.

And now, having shown the way of deliverance from failure, I want to say a little as to the causes of failure in this life of full salvation. The causes do not lie in the strength of the temptation, nor in our own weakness, nor, above all, in any lack in the power or willingness of our Saviour to save us. The promise to Israel was positive, "There shall not any man be able to stand before thee all the days of thy life." And the promise to us is equally positive, "God is faithful, who will not suffer you to be tempted above that ye are able; but will with the' temptation, also make a way of escape that ye may be able to bear it."

The men of Ai were "but few," and yet the people who had conquered the mighty Jericho "fled before the men of Ai." It was not the strength of their enemy, neither had God failed them. The cause of their defeat lay somewhere else, and the Lord Himself declares it, "Israel hath sinned, and they have also transgressed my covenant which I commanded them; for they have even taken of the accursed thing, and have also stolen and dissembled also, and they have put it even among their own stuff. Therefore the children of Israel could not stand before their enemies, but turned their backs upon their enemies." It was a hidden evil that conquered them. Deep down under the earth, in an obscure tent in that vast army, was hidden something against which God had a controversy, and this little hidden thing made the whole army helpless before their enemies. "There is an accursed thing in the midst of thee, O Israel: thou canst not stand before thine enemies until ye take away the accursed thing from among you." The teaching here is simply this, that anything allowed in the heart which is contrary to the will of God, let it seem ever so insignificant, or be ever so deeply hidden, will cause us to fall before our enemies. Any root of bitterness cherished towards another, any self-seeking, any harsh judgments indulged in, any slackness in obeying the voice of the Lord, any doubtful habits or surroundings, any one of these things will effectually cripple and paralyze our spiritual life. We may have hidden the evil in the most remote corner of our hearts, and may have covered it over from our sight, refusing even to recognise its existence—of which, however, we cannot help being all the time secretly aware. We may steadily ignore it, and persist in declarations of consecration and full trust; we may be more earnest than ever in our religious duties, and have the eyes of our understanding opened more and more to the truth and the beauty of the life and walk of faith. We may seem to ourselves and to others to have reached an almost impregnable position of victory, and yet we may find ourselves suffering bitter defeats. We may wonder, and question, and despair, and pray. Nothing will do any good until the accursed thing is dug up from its hiding-place, brought out to the light, and laid before God. And the moment a believer who is walking in this interior life meets with a defeat, he must at once seek for the cause, not in the strength of that particular enemy, but in something behind—some hidden want of consecration lying at the very centre of his being. Just as a head-ache is not the disease itself, but only a symptom of a disease situated in some other part of the body, so the sin in such a Christian is only the symptom of an evil hidden probably in a very different part of his being.

Sometimes the evil may be hidden even in that which, at a cursory glance, would look like good. Beneath apparent zeal for the truth may be hidden a judging spirit, or a subtle leaning to our own understanding. Beneath apparent Christian faithfulness, may be hidden an absence of Christian love. Beneath an apparently rightful care for our affairs, may be hidden a great want of trust in God. I believe our blessed Guide, the indwelling Holy Spirit, is always secretly discovering these things to us by continual little twinges and pangs of conscience, so that we are left without excuse. But it is very easy to disregard His gentle voice, and insist upon it to ourselves that all is right; and thus the fatal evil will continue hidden in our midst, causing defeat in most unexpected .quarters.

A capital illustration of this occurred to me once in my housekeeping. I had moved into a new house, and, in looking over it to see if it was all ready for occupancy, I noticed in the cellar a very clean-looking cider-cask, headed up at both ends. I debated with myself whether I should have it taken out of the cellar and opened, to see what was in it, but concluded, as it seemed empty and looked nice, to leave it undisturbed, especially as it would have been quite a piece of work to get it up the stairs. I did not feel quite easy, but reasoned away my scruples and left it. Every spring and fall, when house-cleaning time came on, I would remember that cask, with a little twinge of my housewifely conscience, feeling that I could not quite rest in the thought of a perfectly cleaned house while it remained unopened; for how did I know but under its fair exterior it contained some hidden evil? Still I managed to quiet my scruples on the subject, thinking always of the trouble it would involve to investigate it; and for two or three years the innocent-looking cask stood quietly in my cellar. Then, most unaccountably, moths began to fill my house. I used every possible precaution against them, and made every effort to eradicate them, but in vain. They increased rapidly, and threatened to ruin everything I had. I suspected my carpets as being the cause, and subjected them to a thorough cleaning. I suspected my furniture, and had it newly upholstered. I suspected all sorts of impossible things. At last the thought of the cask flashed on me. At once I had it brought up out of the cellar, and the head knocked in; and I think it is safe to say that thousands of moths poured out. The previous occupant of the house must have headed it up with something in it which bred moths, and this was the cause of all my trouble.

Now I believe that, in the same way, some innocent looking habit or indulgence—some apparently unimportant and safe thing, about which we yet have, now and then, little twinges of conscience—something which is not brought out fairly into the light, and investigated under the searching eye of God—lies at the root of most of the failure in this higher life. *All* is not given up. Some secret corner is kept locked against the entrance of the Lord. And therefore we cannot stand before our enemies, but find ourselves smitten down in their presence.

It is necessary to keep continually before us this prayer: "Search me, O God, and know my heart; try me, and know my thoughts; and see if there be any wicked way in me, and lead me in the way everlasting" in order to prevent failure, or to discover its cause if we find we have failed.

And now I beg of you, dear Christians, do not think, because I have said all this about failure, that I believe in it. There is no necessity for it whatever. The Lord Jesus *is* able, according to the declaration concerning Him, to deliver us out of the hands of our enemies, that we may "serve Him without fear, in holiness and righteousness before Him all the days of our life."

Let us then pray, every one of us, day and night: "Lord, keep us from sinning, and make us living witnesses of Thy mighty power to save to the uttermost;" and let us never be satisfied until we are so pliable in His hands, and have learned so to trust Him that He will be able to "make us perfect in every good work, to do His will, working in us that which is well pleasing in His sight, through Jesus Christ; to whom be glory for ever and ever. Amen!"

14

DOUBTS

G REAT MANY CHRISTIANS are slaves to the habit of doubting. No drunkard was ever more utterly bound by the chains of his fatal habit than they are by theirs. Every step of their whole Christian life is taken against the fearful odds of an army of doubts, that are for ever lying in wait to assail them at each favourable moment. Their lives are made wretched, their usefulness is effectually hindered, and their communion with God is continually broken by their doubts. And although the entrance of the soul upon the life of faith, of which this book treats, does in many cases take it altogether out of the region where these doubts live and flourish, yet even here it sometimes happens that the old tyrant will rise up and reassert his sway, and will cause the feet to stumble and the heart to fail, even when he cannot succeed in utterly turning the believer back into the dreary wilderness again.

We all of us remember, doubtless, the childish fascination, and yet horror, of that story of Christian's imprisonment in Doubting Castle by the wicked giant Despair, and our exultant sympathy in his escape through those massive gates and from that cruel tyrant. Little did we suspect then that we should ever find ourselves taken prisoner by the same giant, and imprisoned in the same castle. And yet I fear to every member of the Church of Christ there has been at least one such experience. Turn to the account again, if it is not fresh in your minds, and see if you do not see pictured there experiences of your own that have been very grievous to bear at the time, and very sorrowful to look back upon afterwards.

It seems strange that people, whose very name of Believers implies that their one chiefest characteristic is that they believe, should have to confess to such experiences. And yet it is such a universal habit that I feel if the majority of the Church were to be named over again, the only fitting and descriptive name that could be given them would be that of Doubters. In fact, most Christians have settled down under their doubts, as to a sort of inevitable malady, from which they suffer acutely, but to which they must try to be resigned as a part of the necessary discipline of this earthly life. And they lament over their doubts as a man might lament over his rheumatism, making themselves out as an "interesting case" of especial and peculiar trial, which requires the tenderest sympathy and the utmost consideration. And this is too often true of believers, who are earnestly longing to enter upon the life and walk of faith, and who have made perhaps many steps towards it. They have got rid, it may be, of the old .doubts that once tormented them, as to whether their sins are really forgiven, and whether they shall, after all, get safe to Heaven; but they have not got rid of doubting. They have simply shifted the habit to a higher platform. They are saying, perhaps, "Yes, I believe my sins *are* forgiven, and I *am* a child of God through faith in Jesus Christ. I dare not doubt this any more. But then ———." And this *"but then"* includes an interminable array of doubts concerning every declaration and every promise our Father has made to His children. One after another they fight with them and refuse to believe them, until they can have some more reliable proof of their being true, than the simple word of their God. And then they wonder why they are permitted to walk in such darkness, and look upon themselves: almost in the light of martyrs, and groan under the peculiar spiritual conflicts they are compelled to endure.

Spiritual conflicts! Far better would they be named did we call them spiritual rebellions! Our fight is to be a fight of faith, and the moment we doubt, our fight ceases and our rebellion begins.

I desire to put forth, if possible, one vigorous protest against this whole thing.

Just as well might I join in with the laments of a drunkard, and unite with him in prayer for grace to endure the discipline of his fatal appetite, as to give way for one instant to the weak complaints of these enslaved souls, and try to console them under their slavery. To one and to the other I would dare to do nothing else hut proclaim the perfect

114

deliverance the Lord Jesus Christ has in store for them, and beseech, entreat, command them, with all the force of my whole nature, to avail themselves of it and be free. Not for one moment would I listen to their despairing excuses. You ought to be free, you *can* be free, you MUST be free!

Will you undertake to tell me that it is an inevitable necessity for God to be doubted by His children? Is it an inevitable necessity for your children to doubt you? Would you tolerate their doubts a single hour? Would you pity your son, and condole with him, and feel that he was an interesting case, if he should come to you and say, "Father, I cannot believe your word, I cannot trust your love"?

I remember once seeing the indignation of a mother I knew stirred to its very depths by a little doubting on the part of one of her children. She had brought two little girls to my house to leave them while she did some errands. One of them, with the happy confidence of childhood, abandoned herself to all the pleasures she could find in my nursery, and sang and played until her mother's return. The other one, with the wretched caution and mistrust of maturity, sat down alone in a corner *to* wonder whether her mother would remember to come back for her, and to fear she would be forgotten, and to imagine her mother would be glad of the chance to get rid of her anyhow, because she was such a naughty girl; and ended with working herself up into a perfect frenzy of despair. The look on that mother's face, when upon her return the weeping little girl told what was the matter with her, I shall not easily forget. Grief, wounded love, indignation, and pity, all strove together for mastery. But indignation gained the day, and I doubt if that little girl was ever so vigorously dealt with before.

A hundred times in my life since has that scene come up before me with deepest teaching, and has compelled me, peremptorily, to refuse admittance to the doubts about my Heavenly Father's love, and care, and remembrance of me, that have clamoured at the door of my heart for entrance.

I am convinced that to many people doubting is a real luxury, and to deny themselves from indulging in it would be to exercise the hardest piece of self-denial they have ever known. It is a luxury that, like the indulgence in all other luxuries, brings very sorrowful results; and, perhaps, looking at the sadness and misery it has brought into your own Christian experience, you may be tempted to say, "Alas! it is no luxury to me, but only a fearful trial."

But pause for a moment. Try giving it up and you will soon find out whether it is a luxury or not. Do not your doubts come trooping to your door as a company of sympathizing friends, who appreciate your hard case, and have come to condole with you? And is it no luxury to sit down with them and entertain them, and listen to their arguments, and join in with their condolences? "Would it be no self-denial to turn resolutely from them, and refuse to hear a word they bare to say? If you do not know, try it and see.

Have you never tasted the luxury of indulging in hard thoughts against those who have, as you think, injured you? Have you never known what a positive fascination it is to brood over their unkindnesses, and to pry into their malice, and to imagine all sorts of wrong and uncomfortable things about them! It has made you wretched, of course, but it has been a fascinating sort of wretchedness, that you could not easily give up.

And just like this is the luxury of doubting. Things have gone wrong with you in your experience. Dispensations have been mysterious, temptations have been peculiar, your case has seemed different from that of any one's around you. What more natural than to conclude that for some reason God has forsaken you, and does not love you, and is indifferent to your welfare? And how irresistible is the conviction that you are too wicked for Him to care for, or too difficult for Him manage.

You do not mean to blame Him, or accuse Him of injustice, for you feel that His indifference and rejection of you are fully deserved because of your unworthiness. And this very subterfuge leaves you at liberty to indulge in your doubts under the guise of a just and true appreciation of your own shortcomings. But all the while you are as really indulging in hard and wrong thoughts of your Lord as ever you did of a human enemy; for He says He came not to save the righteous, but sinners; and your very sinfulness and unworthiness is your chiefest claim upon His love and His care.

As well might the poor little lamb that has wandered from the flock and got lost in the wilderness say, "The shepherd does not love me, nor care for me, nor remember me, because I am lost. He only loves and cares for the lambs that never wander."

As well might the ill man say, "The doctor will not come to see me, nor give me any medicines, because I am ill. He only cares for and visits well people." Jesus says, "They that are whole need not a physician, but they that are sick." And again He says, "What man of you, having an hundred sheep, if he lose one of them, doth not leave the ninety and nine in the wilderness, and go after that which is lost, until he find it?"

Any thoughts of him, therefore, which are different from what He says of Himself, are hard thoughts, and to indulge in them is far worse than to indulge in hard thoughts of any earthly friend or foe.

From the beginning to the end of your Christian life it is always sinful to indulge in doubts. Doubts are all from the devil, and are always untrue. And the only way to meet them is by a direct and emphatic denial.

And this brings me to the practical part of the whole subject,—as to how to get deliverance from this fatal habit. My answer would be that the deliverance from this can be by no other means than the deliverance from any other sin. It is to be found in Christ and in Him only. You must hand your doubting over to Him as you have learned to hand your other temptations. You must do just what you do with your temper, or your pride. You must *give it up* to the Lord. I believe myself the only effectual remedy is to take a pledge against it, as you would urge a drunkard to do against drink, trusting in the Lord alone to keep you steadfast.

Like any other sin, the stronghold is in the will, and the will to doubt must be surrendered exactly as you surrender the will to yield to any other temptation. God always takes possession of a surrendered will. And if we come to the point of saying that we will not doubt, and surrender this central fortress of our nature to Him, His blessed Spirit will begin at once to work in us all the good pleasure of His will, and we shall find ourselves kept from doubting by His mighty and overcoming power.

The trouble is that in this matter of doubting the soul does not always make a full surrender, but is apt to reserve to itself a little secret liberty to doubt, looking upon it as being sometimes a necessity.

"I do not want to doubt any more," we will say, or, "I hope I shall not;" but it is hard to come to the point of saying, "I will not doubt again." But no surrender is effectual until it reaches the point of saying, "I will not." The liberty to doubt must be given up for ever. And the soul must consent to a continuous life of inevitable trust. It is often necessary, I think, to make a definite transaction of this surrender of doubting, and to come to a point about it. I believe it is quite as necessary in the case of a doubter as in the case of a drunkard. It will not do to give it up by degrees. The total abstinence principle is the only effectual one here.

Then, the surrender once made, the soul must rest absolutely upon the Lord for deliverance in each time of temptation. It must lift up the shield of faith the moment the assault comes. It must hand the very first suggestion of doubt over to the Lord, and must tell Satan to settle the matter with Him. It must refuse to listen to the doubt a single moment. Let it come ever so plausibly, or under whatever guise of humility, the soul must simply say, "I dare not doubt, I must trust. The Lord is good, and HE DOES love me. Jesus saves me; He saves me now." Those three little words, repeated over and over—"Jesus saves me, Jesus saves me"—will put to flight the greatest army of doubts that ever assaulted any soul. I have tried it times without number, and have never known it to fail. Do not stop to argue the matter out with Satan, or to try to convince him that he is wrong. Pay no attention to him whatever; treat him with the utmost contempt. Shut your door in his face, and emphatically deny every word he says to you. Bring up some "It is written," and hurl it after him. Look right at Jesus, and tell Him you trust Him, and you mean to trust Him. Let the doubts clamour as they may, they cannot hurt you if you will not let them in.

I know it will look to you sometimes as though you were shutting the door against your test friends, and your hearts will long after your doubts more than ever the Israelites longed after the flesh-pots of Egypt. But deny yourself; take up your cross in this matter, and unmercifully refuse ever to listen to a single word.

This very day a perfect army of doubts stood awaiting my awaking, and clamoured at my door for admittance. Nothing seemed real, nothing seemed true; and least of all did it seem possible that I— miserable, wretched I— could be the object of the Lord's love, or care, or notice. If I only had been at liberty to let these doubts in, and invite them to take seats and make themselves at home, what a luxury I should have felt it to be! But years ago I made a pledge against doubting, and I would as soon think of violating my pledge against intoxicating liquor as to violate this one. I DARED not admit the first doubt. I therefore lifted up my shield of faith the moment I was conscious of these suggestions, and handing the whole army over to my Lord to conquer, I began to say, over and over, "The blood of Jesus cleanseth me, the blood of Jesus cleanseth me; Jesus saves me, Jesus saves me *now!*" The victory was complete. The enemy had come in like a flood, but the Lord lifted up a standard against him, and he was routed and put to flight; and my soul is singing the song of Moses and the Children of Israel, saying, "I will sing unto the Lord, for He hath triumphed gloriously: the horse and his rider hath He thrown in the sea. The Lord is my strength and my song, and He is become my salvation. The Lord is a man of war; the Lord is His name."

Dear, doubting soul, go and do likewise; and a similar victory shall be thine.

As you lay down this book take up your pen and write out your determination never to doubt again. Make it a real transaction between your soul and the Lord. Give up your liberty to doubt for ever. Put your will in this matter over on the Lord's side, and trust Him to keep you from falling. Tell Him all about your utter weakness and your long encouraged habits of doubt, and how helpless you are before your enemy, and commit the whole battle to Him. Tell Him you will not doubt again; and then henceforward keep your face steadfastly looking unto Jesus, away from yourself and away from your doubts, holding fast the profession of your faith without wavering, because He is faithful who has promised. And as surely as you do thus hold the beginning of your confidence steadfast unto the end, just so surely shall you find yourself in this matter made MORE than conqueror, through Him who loves you.

15

PRACTICAL RESULTS IN THE

DAILY WALK AND

CONVERSATION

I F ALL THAT HAS BEEN said concerning the life hid with Christ in God be true, its results in the practical daily walk and conversation ought to be very marked, and the people who have entered into the enjoyment of it ought to be, in very truth, a peculiar people, zealous of good works.

My dear hoy once wrote to a friend something to this effect: that we are God's witnesses necessarily, because the world will not read the Bible, but they will read our lives; and that upon the report these give will very much depend their belief in the Divine nature of the religion we profess. As a late preacher said, it is an age of facts, and inquiries are being increasingly turned from theories to realities. If our religion is to make any headway now, it must be proved to be more than a theory, and we must present to the investigation of the critical minds of our age, the grand facts of lives which have been actually and manifestly transformed by the mighty power of God working in us all the good pleasure of His will. Give us forms of life, say the Scientists, and we will be convinced. And when the Church is able to present to them in all its members the form of a holy life their last stronghold will be conquered.

I desire, therefore, before closing my book, to speak very solemnly of what I conceive to be the necessary fruits of a life of faith such as I have been describing and to press home to the hearts of every one of my readers their responsibility to walk worthy of the high calling wherewith they have been called.

And I would speak to some of you, at least, as personal friends, for I feel sure we have not gone thus far together through this book without there having grown in your hearts, as there has in mine, a tender personal interest and longing for one another, that we may in everything show forth the praises of Him who has called us out of darkness into His marvellous light. As a friend, then, to friends, I am sure I may speak very plainly, and will be pardoned if I go into some details of our daily lives which may seem of secondary importance, and yet which make up the largest part of them.

The standard of practical holy living has been so low among Christians that the least degree of real devotedness of life and walk is looked upon with surprise, and even often with disapprobation, by a large portion of the Church. And, for the most part, the followers of the Lord Jesus Christ are satisfied with a life so conformed to the world, and so like it in almost every respect, that, to a casual observer, no difference is discernible.

But we, who have heard the call of our God to a life of entire consecration and perfect trust, must do differently from all this. We must come out from the world and be separate, and must not be conformed to it in our characters nor in our lives. We must give up its friendships, its pursuits, its interests. Our conversation must be in Heaven, and we must seek those things that are above, where Christ sitteth on the right hand of God. We must walk through the world as Christ walked. We must have the mind that was in Him. As pilgrims and strangers we must abstain from fleshly lusts that war against the soul. As good soldiers of Jesus Christ, we must disentangle ourselves from the affairs of this life as far as possible, that we may please Him who hath chosen us to be soldiers. We must abstain from all appearance of evil. We must be kind one to another, tender-hearted, forgiving one another, even as God, for Christ's sake, hath forgiven us. We must not resent injuries or unkindness, but must return good for evil, and turn the other cheek to the hand that smites us. We must take always the lowest place among our fellow-men; and seek not our own honour, but the honour of others. We must be gentle, and meek, and yielding; not standing up for our own rights, but for the rights of others. We must do all that we do for the glory of God. And, to sum it all up, since He which hath called us is holy, so must we be holy in *all manner* of conversation; because it is written, "Be ye holy, for I am holy."

Now, dear friends, this is all exceedingly practical, and means, surely, a life very different from the lives of most Christians around us. It means that we do really and absolutely turn our backs on the world and its fashions, and its amusements, and its ways. It means that we are a peculiar people, not only in the eyes of God, but in the eyes of the world around us; and that, wherever we go, it will be known from our habits, our dress; our conversation, and our pursuits, that we are followers of the Lord Jesus Christ, and are not of the world, even as He was not of the world. We shall no longer feel that our money is our own, but the Lord's, to be used in His service. We shall not feel at liberty to use our energies exclusively in the pursuit of worldly means, but, seeking first the kingdom of God and His righteousness, shall have all needful things added unto us. We shall find ourselves forbidden to seek the highest places, or to strain after worldly advantages. We shall not be permitted to be conformed to the world in our dress, nor in our ways of living. We shall not be able to go to balls, and operas, and dances, as the world does. We shall not dare to waste our intellects nor our time in reading the world's novels. Our days will be spent not in serving ourselves, but in serving our Lord; and yet all our rightful duties will be more perfectly performed than ever, because whatever we do will be done "not with eye service as men-pleasers, but as the servants of Christ, doing the will of God from the heart."

Into all these things we shall undoubtedly be led by the blessed Spirit of God, if we give ourselves up to His guidance. But unless we have the right standard of Christian life set before us, we shall be hindered by our ignorance from recognizing His voice; and it is for this reason I desire to be very plain and definite in my statements.

I have noticed that wherever there has been a faithful following of the Lord in a consecrated soul, several things have inevitably followed, sooner or later.

Meekness and quietness of spirit become in time the characteristics of the daily life. A submissive acceptance of the will of God as it comes

123

in the hourly events of each day; pliability in the hands of God to do or to suffer all the good pleasure of His will; sweetness under provocation; calmness in the midst of turmoil and bustle; yieldingness to the wishes of others, and an insensibility to slights and affronts; absence of worry or anxiety; deliverance from care and fear;—all these, and many other similar graces, are invariably found to be the natural outward development of that inward life which is hid with Christ in God. Then as to the habits of life: we always see such Christians sooner or later laying aside their worldly amusements, giving up their novel-reading, putting off their jewelry, dressing in simplicity and without useless ornamentation, renouncing worldly habits, and surrendering all purely fleshly gratifications. Sooner or later I have generally found that smoking is given up, and the drinking of wine or beer, except as a medicine, is surrendered. Dancing is seen to be contrary to the will of God; the opera and the theatre are felt to he places unfit for the presence of a follower of the Lord Jesus. The voice is dedicated to God, to be used in singing His praises. The purse is placed at His disposal. The pen is dedicated to write for Him, the lips to speak for Him, the hands and the feet to do His bidding. Year after year such Christians are seen to grow more unworldly, more heavenly-minded, more transformed, more like Christ, until even their very faces express so much of the beautiful inward Divine life, that all who look at them cannot but take knowledge of them that they live with Jesus, and are abiding in Him.

I feel sure that to each one of you have come at least some Divine intimations or foreshadowings of the life I here describe. Have you not begun to feel dimly conscious of the voice of God speaking to you in the depths of your soul about these things? Has it not been a pain and a distress to you of late to put on some of your jewelry or your fashionable attire? Has not your soul been plunged into inward trouble and doubt about certain amusements or pursuits in which you have been formerly accustomed to indulge? Have you not begun to feel uneasy with some of your habits or ways, and to wish that you could do differently in these respects? Have not paths of devotedness and of service begun to open out before you with the longing thought, "Oh, that I could walk in them!"

All these longings and doubts, and this inward distress, are the voice of the Good Shepherd in your heart seeking to call you out of all that is contrary to His will, Oh! let me entreat of you not to turn .away from His gentle pleadings. You little know the sweet paths into which He means to lead you by these very steps, nor the wonderful stores of blessedness that lie at their end, or you would spring forward with an eager joy to yield to every one of His requirements. The heights of Christian perfection can only be reached by faithfully each moment following the Guide who is to lead you there, and He reveals your way to you one step at a time, in the little things of your daily lives, asking only on your part that you yield yourselves up to His guidance. If, then, in anything you feel doubtful or troubled, be sure that it is the voice of your Lord, and surrender it at once to His bidding, rejoicing with a great joy that He has begun thus to lead and guide you. Be perfectly pliable in His dear hands, go where He entices you, turn away from all from which He makes you shrink, obey Him perfectly, and He will lead you out swiftly and easily into a wonderful life of conformity to Himself, that will be a testimony to all around you, beyond what you yourself will ever know.

I knew a soul thus given up to follow the Lord whithersoever He might lead her, who in three short months travelled from the depths of darkness and despair into the realisation and conscious experience of the most blessed union with the Lord Jesus Christ. Out of the midst of her darkness she consecrated herself to the Lord, surrendering her will up altogether to Him, that He might work in her to will and to do of His own good pleasure. Immediately He began to speak to her by His Spirit in her heart, suggesting to her some little acts of service for Him, and troubling her about certain things in her habits and her life—her jewelry, her dress, her singing, her reading, her amusements. She recognised His voice, and yielded to Him each thing He asked for, even those about which she only felt doubtful, realising that it was safer to put the benefit of the doubt on the Lord's side, than to run the risk of disobeying Him.

He led her rapidly on, day by day conforming her more and more to His will, and making her life such a testimony to those around her, that even some who had begun by opposing and disbelieving were forced to acknowledge that it was of God, and were won to a similar surrender. And, finally, after three short months of this faithful following it came to pass, so swiftly had she gone, that her Lord was able to reveal to her wondering soul the deepest secrets of His love, and to fulfil to her the marvellous promise of John 14:21 and 23, by coming unto her, and making His abode with her. Think you she has ever regretted her whole-hearted following of Him? Or that aught but thankfulness and joy can ever fill her soul when she reviews the steps by which her feet have been led to this place of wondrous blessedness, even though some of them may have seemed at the time hard to take? Ah, dear soul, if thou wouldst know a like blessing, abandon thyself, like her, to the guidance of thy dearest Lord, and shrink from no surrender for which He may call.

"The perfect way is hard to flesh,
It is not hard to love;
If thou wert sick for want of God,
How swiftly wouldst thou move!"

Surely thou canst trust Him! And if some things may be called for which look to thee of but little moment, and not worthy thy Lord's attention, remember that He sees not as man seeth, and that things small to thee may be in His eyes the key and the clue to the deepest springs of thy being. In order to mould thee into entire conformity to His will, He must have thee pliable in His hands, and this pliability is more quickly reached by yielding in the little things than even by the greater. Thy one great desire is to follow Him fully; canst thou not say then a continual "Yes" to all His sweet commands, whether small or great, and trust Him to lead thee by the shortest road to thy fullest blessedness?

My dear friend, this, and nothing less than this, is what thy consecration meant, whether thou knew it or not. It meant *inevitable* obedience. It meant that the will of thy God was henceforth to be thy will under all circumstances and at all times. It meant that from that moment thou surrendered thy liberty of choice, and gave thyself up utterly into the control of thy Lord. It meant an hourly following of Him whithersoever He might lead thee, without any dream of turning back.

And now I appeal to thee to make good thy word. Let everything else go, that thou mayst live out, in a practical daily walk and conversation, the Christ-life thou hast dwelling within thee. Thou art united to thy Lord by a wondrous tie; walk, then, as He walked, and show to the unbelieving world the blessed reality of His mighty power to save, by letting Him save *thee* to the very uttermost. Thou needst not fear to consent to this, for He is thy Saviour, and His power is to do it all. He is not asking thee, in thy poor weakness, to do it thyself; He only asks thee to yield thyself to Him, that He may work in thee to will and to do by His own mighty power. Thy part is to yield thyself, His part is to work; and never, never will He give thee any command which is not accompanied by ample power to obey it. Take no thought for the morrow in this matter; but abandon thyself with a generous trust to thy loving Lord, who has promised never to call His own sheep out into any path without Himself going before them to make the way easy and safe. Take each little step as He makes it plain to thee. Bring all thy life in each of its details to Him to regulate and guide. Follow gladly and quickly the sweet suggestions of His Spirit in thy soul. And day by day thou wilt find Him bringing thee more and more into conformity with His will in all things; moulding thee and fashioning thee, as thou art able to bear it, into a vessel unto His honour, sanctified and meet for His use, and fitted to every good work. So shall be given to thee the sweet joy of being an epistle of Christ known and read of all men; and thy light shall shine so brightly that men seeing, not thee, but thy good works, shall glorify, not thee, but thy Father which is in Heaven.

"And it shall come to pass, if thou shalt hearken diligently unto the voice of the Lord thy God, to observe and to do all His commandments which I command thee this day, that the Lord thy God will set thee on high above all nations of the earth; and all these blessings shall come on thee, and overtake thee, if thou shalt hearken unto the voice of the Lord thy God.

"Blessed shalt thou be in the city, and blessed shalt thou be in the field.

"Blessed shall be the fruit of thy body, and the fruit of thy ground, and the fruit of thy cattle, the increase of thy kine, and the flocks of thy sheep.

"Blessed shall be thy basket and thy store.

"Blessed shalt thou be when thou comest in, and blessed shalt thou be when thou goest out.

"The Lord shall cause thine enemies that rise up against thee to be smitten before thy face; they shall come out against thee one way, and flee before thee seven ways.

"The Lord shall command the blessing upon thee in thy storehouses, and in all that thou settest thine hand unto; and He shall bless thee in the land which the Lord thy God giveth thee.

"The Lord shall establish thee an holy people unto Himself, as He hath sworn unto thee, if thou shalt keep the commandments of the Lord thy God, and walk in His ways.

"And all people of the earth shall see that thou art called by the name of the Lord, and they shall be afraid of thee.

"And the Lord shall make thee plenteous in goods, in the fruit of thy body, and in the fruit of thy cattle-, in the fruit of thy ground, in the land which the Lord sware unto thy fathers to give thee.

"And the Lord shall make thee the head, and not the tail; and thou shalt be above only, and thou shalt not be beneath; if that thou hearken unto the commandments of the Lord thy God, which I command thee this day, to observe and to do them."

16

THE JOY OF OBEDIENCE

I REMEMBER READING ONCE somewhere this sentence, "Perfect obedience would be perfect happiness, if only we had perfect confidence in the power we were obeying." I remember being struck with the saying, as the revelation of a possible, although hitherto undreamed of, way of happiness; and often afterwards, through all the lawlessness and wilfulness of my life, did that saying recur to me as the vision of a rest, and yet of a possible development, that would soothe and at the same time satisfy all my yearnings.

Need I say that this rest has been revealed to me now, not as a vision, but as a reality; and that I have seen in the Lord Jesus, the Master to whom we may all yield up our implicit obedience, and, taking His yoke upon us, may find our perfect rest.

You little know, dear hesitating soul, of the joy you, are missing. The Master has revealed Himself to you, and is calling for your complete surrender, and you shrink and hesitate. A measure of surrender you are willing to make, and think indeed it is fit and proper you should. But an *utter* abandonment, without any reserves, seems to you too much to be asked for. You are afraid of it. It involves too much, you think, and is too great a risk. To be measurably obedient you desire, to be perfectly obedient appals you.

And then, too, you see other souls who seem able to walk with easy consciences, in a far wider path than that which appears to be marked out for you, and you ask yourself why this need be. It seems strange, and perhaps hard to you, that you must do what they need not and must leave undone what they have liberty to do.

Ah! dear Christian, this very difference between you, is your privilege, though you do not yet know it. Your Lord says, "He that *hath* my commandments, and keepeth them, he it is that loveth Me; and he that loveth Me shall be loved of my Father, and I will love him, and will manifest Myself to him." You *have* His commandments; those you envy, have them not. *You* know the mind of your Lord about many things, in which, as yet, *they* are walking in darkness. Is not this a privilege? Is it a cause for regret that your soul is brought into such near and intimate relations with your Master, that He is able to tell you things which those who are further oft may not know? Do you not realize what a tender degree of intimacy is implied in this?

There are many relations in life which require from the different parties only very moderate degrees of devotion. "We may have really pleasant friendships with one another, and yet spend a large part of our lives in separate interests, and widely differing pursuits. When together, we may greatly enjoy one another's society, and find many congenial points; but separation is not any especial distress to us, and other and more intimate friendships do not interfere. There is not enough love between us to give us either the right or the desire to enter into and share one another's most private affairs. A certain degree of reserve and distance, is the suitable thing we feel. But there are other relations in life where all this is changed. The friendship becomes love. The two hearts give themselves to one another, to be no longer two but one. A union of souls takes place, which makes all that belongs to one the property of the other. Separate interests and separate paths in life are no longer possible. Things which were lawful before become unlawful now, because of the nearness of the tie that binds. The reserve and distance suitable to mere friendship become fatal in love. Love gives all, and must have all in return. The wishes of one become binding obligations to the other, and the deepest desire of each heart is that it may know every secret wish or longing of the other, in order that it may fly on the wings of the wind to gratify it.

Do such as these chafe under this yoke which love imposes? Do they envy the cool, calm, reasonable friendships they see around them, and regret the nearness into which their souls are brought to their beloved one, because of the obligations it creates? Do they not rather glory in these very obligations, and inwardly pity, with a tender yet exulting joy, the poor far-off ones who dare not come so near? Is not

130

every fresh revelation of the mind of one another a fresh delight and privilege, and is any path found hard which their love compels them to travel?

Ah! dear souls, if you have ever known this even for a few hours in any earthly relation; if you have ever loved a fellow human being enough to find sacrifice and service on their behalf a joy; if a whole-souled abandonment of your will to the will of another, has ever gleamed across you as a blessed and longed-for privilege, or as a sweet and precious reality, then by all the tender longing love of your heavenly Master, would I entreat you to let it be so towards Christ!

He loves you with more than the love of friendship. As a bridegroom rejoices over his bride, so does He rejoice over you, and nothing but a full surrender will satisfy Him. He has given you all, and He asks for all in return. The slightest reserve will grieve Him to the heart. He spared not Himself, and how can you spare yourself? For your sake He poured out in a lavish abandonment all that He had, and for His sake you must pour out all that you have without stint or measure.

Oh, be generous in your self-surrender! Meet His measureless devotion for you, with a measureless devotion to Him. Be glad and eager to throw yourself headlong into His dear arms, and to hand over the reins of government to Him. "Whatever there is of you, let Him have it all. Give up for ever everything that is separate from Him. Consent to resign from this time forward all liberty of choice; and glory in the blessed nearness of union which makes this enthusiasm of devotedness not only possible but necessary. Have you never longed to lavish your love and attentions upon some one far off from you in position or circumstances, with whom you were not intimate enough to dare to approach them? Have you not felt a capacity for self-surrender and devotedness that has seemed to bum within you like a fire, and yet had no object upon which it dared to lavish itself? Have not your hands been full of alabaster boxes of ointment, very precious, which you have never been near enough to any heart to pour out? If, then, you are hearing the sweet voice of your Lord calling you into a place of nearness to Himself, which will require a separation from all else, and which will make an enthusiasm of devotedness not only possible, but necessary, will you shrink or hesitate? Will you think it hard that He reveals to you more of His mind than He does to others, and that He will not allow you to be happy in anything which separates you from Himself? Do you *want* to go where He cannot go with you, or to have pursuits which He cannot share?

No! no, a thousand times no! You will spring out to meet His dear will with an eager joy. Even His slightest wish will become a binding law to you, which it would fairly break your heart to disobey. You will glory in the very narrowness of the path He marks out for you, and will pity with an infinite pity the poor far off ones who have missed this precious joy. The obligations of love will be to you its sweetest privileges; and the right you have acquired to lavish the uttermost abandonment of all that you have upon your Lord, will seem to lift you into a region of unspeakable glory. The perfect happiness of perfect obedience mil dawn upon your soul, and you mil begin to know something of what Jesus meant when He said, "I *delight* to do Thy will O my God."

And do you think the joy in this will be all on your side? Has the Lord no joy in those who have thus .surrendered themselves to Him, and who love to obey Him? Ah, my friends, we are not fit to speak of this; but surely the Scriptures reveal to us glimpses of the delight, the satisfaction, the joy our Lord has in us, that ravish the soul with their marvellous suggestions of blessedness. That *we* should need Him, is easy to comprehend! that *He* should need us, seems incomprehensible. That our desire should be towards Him, is a matter of course; but that His desire should be towards us, passes the bounds of human belief. And yet,—and yet He says it, and what can we do but believe Him? He has made our hearts capable of this supreme over-mastering affection, and has offered Himself as the object of it. It is infinitely precious to Him, and in tenderest accents He is saying to each one of us, as He said to Peter, "Lovest thou Me; lovest thou Me more than these." Continually at every heart He is knocking, asking to be taken in as the supreme object of love. "Wilt thou have Me," He says to the believer, "to be thy Beloved? Wilt thou follow Me into suffering and loneliness, and endure hardness for my sake, and ask for no reward but My smile of approval, and My word of praise? Wilt thou throw thyself with an utter abandonment into My will? Wilt thou give up to Me the absolute control of thyself and all that thou art? Wilt thou be content with pleasing Me and Me only? May I have My way with thee in all things? Wilt thou come into so close a union with Me as to make a separation from the world necessary? Wilt thou accept Me for thy only Lord, and leave all others to cleave only unto ME?"

In a thousand ways He makes this offer of union with Himself to every believer. But all do not say "Yes" to Him. Other loves and other interests seem to them too precious to be cast aside. They do not miss of Heaven because of this. But they miss an unspeakable joy.

You, however, are not one of these. From the very first your soul has cried out eagerly and gladly to all His offers, "Yes, Lord; yes!" You are more than ready to pour out upon Him all your richest treasures of love and devotedness. You have brought to Him an enthusiasm of self-surrender that perhaps may disturb and distress the more prudent and moderate Christians around you. Your love makes necessary a separation from the world, which a lower love cannot even conceive of. Sacrifices and services are possible and sweet to you, which could not come into the grasp of a more half-hearted devotedness. The union upon which you have entered gives you the right to a lavish outpouring of your *all* upon your beloved One. Services of which more distant souls know nothing, become now your sweetest and most joyful privilege. Your Lord claims from you, because of your union with Him, far more than He claims of them. What to them is lawful, love has made unlawful for you. To you He can make known His secrets, and to you He looks for an instant response to every requirement of His love.

Oh, it is wonderful! the glorious unspeakable privilege upon which you have entered! How little it will matter to you if men shall hate you, or shall separate you from their company, and shall reproach you and cast out your name as evil for His dear sake! You may well rejoice in that day and leap for joy; for behold, your reward is great in Heaven; and if you are a partaker of His suffering, you shall he also of His glory.

In you He is seeing of the travail of His soul, and is satisfied. Your love and devotedness are His precious reward for all He has done for you. It is unspeakably sweet to Him. Do not be afraid then to let yourself go in a heart-whole devotedness to your Lord that can brook *no* reserves. Others may not approve, but He will, and that is enough. Do not stint or measure your obedience or your service. Let your heart and your hand be as free to serve Him, as His heart and hand were to serve you. Let Him have all there is of you—body, soul, and spirit, time, talents, voice—everything. Lay your whole life open before Him, that He may control it. Say to Him each day, "Lord, how shall I regulate this day so as to please Thee? Where shall I go? What shall I do? Whom shall I visit? What shall I say?" Give your dress up into His control and say, "Lord, tell me how to dress so as to please Thee?" Give Him your reading, your pursuits, your friendships, and say, "Lord, speak to me about all these, and tell me just what Thy mind is about them." Do not let there be a day nor an hour in which you are not consciously doing His will, and following Him wholly. And this personal service to Him will give a halo to your life, and gild the most monotonous existence with a heavenly glow. Have you ever grieved that the romance of youth is so soon lost in the hard realities of the world? Bring Christ thus into your life and into all its details, and a far grander enthusiasm will thrill your soul, than the brightest days of youth could ever know, and nothing will seem hard or stern again. The meanest life will be glorified by this. Often, as I have watched a poor woman at her washtub, and have thought of all the disheartening accessories of such a life, and have been tempted to wonder why such lives need to be, there has come over me, with a thrill of joy, the recollection of this possible glorification of it, and I have said to myself, even this life, lived in Christ, and with Christ, following Him whithersoever He may lead, would be filled with a spiritual enthusiasm that would make every hour of it glorious. And I have gone on my way comforted to know that God's most wondrous blessings thus lie in the way of the poorest and the meanest lives. "For," says our Lord Himself, "whosoever," whether they be rich or poor, old

134

or young, bond or free, "whosoever shall do the will of God, the same is my brother, and. my sister, and my mother."

Pause a moment over these simple yet amazing words. His brother, and sister, and mother! "What would we not have given to have been one of these! Oh, let me entreat of you, beloved Christian, to come taste and see for yourself how good the Lord is, and 'what wonderful things He has in store for those who keep His commandments, and who do those things that are pleasing in His sight."

"So they read in the book in the law of God distinctly, and gave the sense, and caused them to understand the reading.

"And Nehemiah, which is the Tirshatha, and Ezra the priest the scribe, and the Levites that taught the people, said unto all the people, This day is holy unto the Lord your God; mourn not, nor weep. For all the people wept, when they heard the words of the law.

"Then he said unto them, Go your way, eat the fat, and drink the sweet, and send portions unto them for whom nothing is prepared: for this day is holy unto our Lord: neither be ye sorry; for the joy of the Lord is your strength.

"So the Levites stilled all the people, saying, Hold your peace, for the day is holy; neither be ye grieved.

"And all the people went their way to eat, and to drink, and to send portions, and to make great mirth, because they had understood the words that were declared unto them."

17

THE JOY OF UNION

ALL THE DEALINGS of God with the soul of the believer are in order to bring it into oneness with Himself, that the prayer of our Lord may be fulfilled—"That they all may be one; as Thou, Father, art in me and I in Thee, that they also may be one in us." . . . "I in them, and Thou in me, that they may be made perfect in one, and that the world may know that Thou hast sent me, and hast loved them as Thou hast loved me."

This soul-union was the glorious purpose in the heart of God for His people before the foundation of the world. It was the mystery hid from ages and generations. It was accomplished in the death of Christ. It has been made known by the Scriptures. And it is realised as an actual experience by many of God's dear children.

But not by all. It is true of all, and God has not hidden it or made it hard, but the eyes of many are too dim and their hearts too unbelieving, and they fail to grasp it. And it is for the very purpose of bringing them into the personal and actual realisation of this, that the Lord is stirring up believers everywhere at the present time to abandon themselves to Him, that He may work in them all the good pleasure of His will.

All the previous steps in the Christian life lead up to this. The Lord has made us for it; and until we have intelligently apprehended it, and have voluntarily consented to embrace it, the travail of His soul for us is not satisfied, nor have our hearts found their destined and final rest.

The usual course of Christian experience is pictured in the history of the Disciples. First they were awakened to see their condition and their need, and they came to Christ, and gave in their allegiance to Him. Then they followed Him, worked for Him, believed in Him; and yet how unlike Him! Seeking to be set up one above the other; running away from the cross; misunderstanding His mission and His words; forsaking their Lord in time of danger. But still sent out to preach, recognised by Him as His disciples, possessing power to work for Him. They knew Christ only "after the flesh," as outside of them, their Lord and Master, but not yet their Life.

Then came Pentecost, and these same disciples came to know Him as inwardly revealed; as one with them in actual union—their very indwelling Life. Henceforth He was to them Christ within, working in them to will and to do of His good pleasure, delivering them by the law of the Spirit of His life from the bondage to the law of sin and death under which they had been held. No longer was it between themselves and Him a war of wills and a clashing of interest. One will alone animated them, and that was His will. One interest alone was dear to them, and that was His. They were made ONE with Him.

And surely all can recognise this picture, though perhaps as yet the final stage of it has not been fully reached. You may have left much to follow Christ, dear reader; you may have believed on Him, and worked for Him, and loved Him, and yet may not be like Him. Allegiance you know, and confidence you know, but not yet union. There are two wills, two interests, two lives. You have not yet lost your own life that you may live only in His. Once it was I and not Christ. Then it was I and Christ. Perhaps now it is even Christ and I. But has it come yet to be Christ only, and not I at all?

If not, shall I tell you how it may? If you have followed me through all the previous chapters in this book, you will surely now be ready to take the final step of faith which will lead your soul out of self and into Christ, and will be prepared to abide in Him for ever, and to know no life but His.

All you need therefore is, to understand what the Scriptures teach about this marvellous union, that you may be sure it is really intended for you.

If you read such passages as 1 Cor. 3:16, "Know ye not that ye are the temple of God, and that the Spirit of God dwelleth in you," and then look at the opening of the chapter to see to whom these wonderful words are spoken, even to "babes in Christ," who were "yet carnal," and walked according to man, you will see that this soul-union of which I speak, this unspeakably glorious mystery of an indwelling God, is the possession of even the weakest and most failing believer in Christ. So that it is not a *new* thing you are to ask for, but only to realise that which you already have. Of every believer in the Lord Jesus it is absolutely true, that his "body is the temple of the Holy Ghost, which is in him, which he has of God."

But although this is true, it is also equally true that unless the believer knows it, and lives in the power of it, it is to him as though it were not. Like the treasures under a man's field, which existed there before they were known or used by him, so does the life of Christ dwell in each believer as really before he knows it and lives in it, as it does afterward, although its power is not manifested until intelligently and voluntarily the believer ceases from his own life, and accepts Christ's life in its place.

It seems to me just in this way. As though Christ were living in a house, shut up in a far-off closet, unknown and unnoticed by the dwellers in the house, longing to make Himself known to them and be one with them in all their daily lives, and share in all their interests: but unwilling to force Himself upon their notice, as nothing but a voluntary companionship could meet or satisfy the needs of His love. The days pass by over that favoured household, and they remain in ignorance of their marvellous privilege. They come and go about all their daily affairs with no thought of their wonderful Guest. Their plans are laid without reference to Him. His wisdom to guide, and His strength to protect, are all lost to them. Lonely days and weeks are spent in sadness, which might have been full of the sweetness of His presence.

But suddenly the announcement is made—"The Lord is in the house!"

How will its owner receive the intelligence? Will he call out an eager thanksgiving, and throw wide open every door for the entrance of his glorious Guest? Or will he shrink and hesitate, afraid of His presence, and seek to reserve some private corner for a refuge from His all-seeing eye?

Dear friend, I make the glad announcement to thee that the Lord is in thy heart. Since the day of thy conversion He has been dwelling there, but thou hast lived on in ignorance of it. Every moment during all that time might have been passed in the sunshine of His sweet presence, and every step have been taken under His advice. But because thou knew it not, and hast never looked for Him there, thy life has been lonely and full of failure. But now that I make the announcement to thee, how wilt thou receive it? Art thou glad to have Him? "Wilt thou throw wide open every door to welcome Him in? Wilt thou joyfully and thankfully give up the government of thy life into His hands? Wilt thou consult Him about everything, and let Him decide each step for thee, and mark out every path? Wilt thou invite Him into thy innermost chambers, and make Him the sharer in thy most hidden life? Wilt thou say, "Yes" to all His longing for union with thee, and with a glad and eager abandonment hand thyself and all that concerns thee over into His hands? If thou wilt, then shall thy soul begin to know something of the joy of union with Christ.

And yet, after all, this is but a faint picture of the blessed reality. For far more glorious than it would be to have Christ a dweller in the house or in the heart, is it to be brought into such a real and actual union with. Him as to be one with Him—one will, one purpose, one interest, one life. Human words cannot express such a glory as this. And yet I *want* to express it. I want to make your souls so unutterably hungry to realise it, that day or night you cannot rest without it. Do you *understand* the words—one with Christ? Do you catch the slightest glimpse of their marvellous meaning? Does not your whole soul begin to exult over such a wondrous destiny? For it is a reality. It means to have no life but His life, to have no will but His will, to have no interests but His interests, to share His riches, to enter into His joys, to partake of His sorrows, to manifest His life, to have the same mind as He had, to think, and feel, and act, and walk as He did. Oh, who could have dreamed that such a destiny could have been ours!

"Wilt thou have it, dear soul? Thy Lord will not force it on thee, for He wants thee as His companion and His friend, and a forced union would be incompatible with this. It must be voluntary on thy part. The bride must say a willing "Yes" to her bridegroom, or the joy of their union is utterly wanting. Canst thou say a willing "Yes" to thy Lord?

It is such a simple transaction and yet so real! The steps are but three. First, be convinced that the Scriptures teach this glorious indwelling of thy God; then surrender thy whole being to Him to be possessed by Him, and finally believe that He *has* taken possession, and *is* dwelling in thee. Begin to reckon thyself dead, and to reckon Christ as thy only life. Maintain this attitude of soul unwaveringly. Say, "I am crucified with Christ, nevertheless I live, yet not I, but Christ liveth in me," over and over day and night, until it becomes the habitual breathing of thy soul. Put off thy self-life by faith continually, and put on the life of Christ. Let this act become, by its constant repetition, the attitude of thy whole being. And as surely as thou dost this day by day, thou shalt find thyself continually bearing about in thy body the dying of the Lord Jesus, that the life also of Jesus may be made manifest in thy mortal flesh. Thou shalt learn to know what salvation means; and shalt have opened out to thy astonished gaze secrets of the Lord, of which thou hast hitherto hardly dreamed.

"As it is written, Eye hath not seen, nor ear heard, neither have entered into the heart of man the things which God hath prepared for them that love Him. But God hath revealed them unto us by His Spirit: for the Spirit searcheth all things, yea, the deep things of God." (1 Cor. 2:9, 10.)

THE END.

Printed in Great Britain
by Amazon

35386578R00081